BUMBLEBEES CAN FLY!

BOOK II

*Inherent Power and Inherent Resiliency
Paradigm for Systematic Development
and Nurturing of Resiliency in
Young Men of Color and Others*

Oscar J. Dowdell-Underwood Ph.D.

Ordering Information:

For orders and inquiries, please contact:
1-888-375-9818
www.toplinkpublishing.com
bookorder@toplinkpublishing.com

Printed in the United States of America

Table Of Contents

Dedication

The World Needs kids and adults, regardless of gender of culture, who understand the power and necessity of knowing how to bounce back in life and to embrace personal, inherent power in order to be proactive in doing every-day life!

This book is dedicated first of all to my Lord and Savior, Jesus Christ, Who gave me the grace to put my passion into words that will change the future of all humanity, including the young men of color whose plight in pursuit of the fulfillment of personal potential and destiny, have been opposed by unprecedented adversity, both internally and externally. It is my hope that all who read this book will discover their own inherent power and inherent resilience, like the bumblebee, to fly in life in spite of the obstacles and challenges that they face. It is my hope that stakeholders who are fortunate to be touched by the bumblebee and inherent power and inherent resiliency paradigm will be passionate about applying its methodology so that all people, including young men of color can learn to be resilient and empowered in their personal living. It is also dedicated to my friend and wife Helen, who is an extraordinary woman of God.

I also dedicate this book to all of my children, godchildren, and spiritual children who have had to sacrifice so much, for you are the family that God gave me as a bonus for my unselfish sharing of myself with humanity. Finally, I dedicate this book to the thousands of students, from pre-k to senior citizens, who taught me how to empower humanity to be resilient in response to adversity and to use failure, disappointment, and setbacks in life as incredible opportunities to achieve in academics and thrive in life.

ABOUT THE BOOK

Bumblebees Can Fly is a conversation with the potential of all of humanity, male and female, of all cultures, but in particular, Young Men of Color, especially Black and Brown young men, who because of the great challenges that come with their being, there is an urgent need for them to become increasingly aware of the deep deposits of resiliency that is in them because of the great adversity that is part and parcel of being young men of color in America and in other parts of the world. It is important to note that human potential strategies that hold great promises for those who face the greatest adversity also works for those who face the least adversity. Why? Because all humanity is gifted with inherent power; therefore, where there is a history of adversity, there is also the presence of inherent resiliency.

Psychological resilience which influences personal thoughts, emotions, perception, and choices, have the power to cause humanity, specifically, Young Men of Color, to counter adversity with resiliency, quickly, effectively, and constructively. It is only by adopting a person-centric personal paradigm for responding to adversity can young men of color begin to systematically tap into their Inherent Power and Inherent Resiliency, and thus, like the bumblebee, respond to that adversity with greater achievement and success in spite of the things that appear to be working against them, but in actuality are working for them.

Bumblebees Can Fly is a needed conversation about the traditionally ignored person-centric assets that people possess, who face great adversity in life. Inherent Power is theirs by their humanity; Inherent Resiliency is theirs by their experiences with adversity.

THE BUMBLEBEE AND HUMANITY'S INTENTIONAL RESILIENCE

"Young Men of Color are not aliens; they, too, are part of humanity. Therefore, what improves their lives, also has the power to improve the lives of the rest of humanity, regardless of race, gender, economics or culture."

R esilience: Personal Power and Personal Strength that resides in the person. Resilience is the ability to bounce back, rebound, and come back from adversity, stronger, healthier, and better than before the opposition or challenge; however, resilience works best when it is the result of a personal policy that is not haphazard or random in response to various adverse events.

Bumblebees Can Fly focuses on personal strength and personal resources that every human being, including Young Men of Color possess by virtue of their humanity, despite their formidable challenges of discrimination, marginalization, and disenfranchisement in life.

In Bumblebees Can Fly, Dr. Oscar Dowdell-Underwood challenges Young Men of Color, as well as parents, educators, churches, government, policymakers, community leaders, and nonprofit organizations to expand opportunity for Young Men of Color and other marginalized people by using their Inherent Power and Personal Resiliency to adopt a SYSTEMATIC PROTOCOL by which they can effectively overcome life challenges by recognizing the strength and resilience that is a major component of the Inherent Power that all people, by virtue of their humanity, possess without needing to seek approval of others.

Transformational living is an intentional use of one's personal inherent power and inherent resilience to change and override any limitations; and, to bounce back from any setbacks or failures in life that prohibit maximum living, maximum achievement and maximum success. Inherent power is defined as an authority to possess a power to be a thing or do a thing without that power having to come from another. By definition, inherent power is also inherent resilience. Through the vast resources and transformative nature of personal inherent power and resilience, all human beings, regardless of ethnicity or economics, regardless of the challenges and obstacles that seem to be erected against them, have the power to change any and everything about them or their lives that don't allow them to be all or live all that God purposed and intended for them.

Being human is synonymous with having to face enormous challenges in life; in fact, we all have something that works against our potential, success, achievement, and the realization of our dreams. Resilience in the Bumblebee is argued in regards to the person-centric paradigm for finally stopping the endless of bleeding of Young Men of Color. Despite its heavy and large body, the bumblebee is able to fly-defying the Law of Aerodynamics. The bumblebee flies because its' Inherent Power and Inherent Resilience, due to intentional adversity that it faces as a way of life, is greater than its challenges, aerodynamics and gravity, included. Supplying resources such as mentoring, tutoring, financial assistance, success counseling, and others has proven to be valuable strategies in addressing underserved students challenges, but the current plight of African American men and other young men of color, and others reminds us that more is needed. The bumblebee and intentional resilience paradigm calls for the developing and embracing an awareness of empowerment in order to face the various challenges in life from a systematic personal power and personal resilience paradigm that focuses on these two things as incredible assets that override any limitations that might impede academic achievement or life success.

As proven by a study group of African American young men at a Midwestern university who taught me that any economic system that emphasizes supply of what appears to be lacking, yet ignores the possession of personal assets that can be used to help address the need, has not and will not create desired results. As with the bumblebee, it flies in spite of the physical attributes that the law of aerodynamics and other physical laws say that it lacks. The bumblebee has been flying or levitating for eons because the demand placed on the inherent power and inherent resilience in it is greater than the force of the adversity and challenges working against it. The same is true of humanity, including young men of color, regardless of the severity of the obstacles and challenges that one may face. In explaining what made the greatest difference in the study group's ability to persist and remain in postsecondary education, and to succeed in life, these young men said that it boiled down to a decision, even under duress and pressure, to summon their inherent power and personal resilience to bounce back from failure, disappointments, and setbacks with a FINAO (Failure is Not An Option) determination to achieve in spite of the conditions and statistics that said it could not be done.

What the study group described was the experience of the bumblebee; for despite its big, heavy body, it is able to fly when the law of aerodynamics says that it is impossible for a bumblebee to fly. The bumblebee flies not because its challenges allow it to, but because the inherent power in it is greater than the challenges, even the law of aerodynamics that work against it. Not only does the bumblebee have inherent power and inherent resilience, but more importantly, all of humanity, including young men of color, possesses it. Inherent power is an authority possessed without it being derived from another. Inherent resiliency, like inherent power, is a right, ability, or faculty of doing a thing, without receiving that right, ability or faculty from another, whether it is people, challenges, or conditions. Just as with all bumblebees, this power is not just in some people, but in all people. In reality, inherent power and resiliency to overcome life obstacles and limitations in order to be, do, have, live, and succeed is an inalienable right that is part of one's humanity.

CHAPTER ONE

RESILIENCE, INHERENT POWER AND THE BUMBLEBEE ANALOGY

Only that which is intentional can truly receive instruction.
Leo Tolstoy said, "Everyone thinks of changing the world,
but no one thinks of changing himself" (Bender, 2002).

Discussions about the needed strategies to effectively answer the plight of Young Men of Color have basically centered around supply of additional resources as opposed to acknowledging the need to place personal demand on internal, personal assets that are already present in them by virtue of their humanity, and historical, personal adversity. Consistently, research points out that despite generational poverty or the absence of desired family support, young men of color and others who have faced great challenges and adversity, can achieve in academics and succeed in life if their awareness of personal inherent power and personal inherent resiliency are greater than perceptions of marginalization, disenfranchisement, and victimization.

According to natural law, in particular, the law of aerodynamics, bumblebees should not be able to fly. But in actuality, the bumblebee demonstrates the power and resilience inherent in them that overcomes even the natural laws, struggles, and challenges that work against them. Resilience is the ability, system, and protocol that is employed to face adversity, trauma, tragedy, threats, or extreme stress and "bouncing back" successfully without becoming too negatively affected by the experience. According to natural law, bumblebees should not be able to fly because their weight and wings theoretically cannot generate enough lift to fly. Experts for years have pondered why the bumblebee flies despite all of the reasons that it should not be able to. The answer is obvious: what is in the bumblebee—its inherent power—is greater than what may work against it.

Bumblebees Can Fly offers a new paradigm for positively addressing the plethora of ways that African-American boys are disproportionately and negatively impacted in America; whether, it be through educational, employment, social, judicial, inequity and disenfranchisement.

Much has been written to address the plight of Young Men of Color; however, through the analogy of the Bumblebee, Bumblebees Can Fly goes beyond merely discussing the problem, but also offers person-centric strategies for Young Men of Color to overcome the formidable challenges in life that threaten their very survival.

If bumblebees can fly, and they can and have been doing so for eons, then most certainly, black and other young men of color can overcome their obstacles and challenges, whether racial, economic, violence, historical discrimination or marginalization, etc., and live successful and productive lives. My research, explained in my book, *Burden of Hope*, endeavored to examine the reasons why some young African American men succeed at institutions of higher learning as opposed to why others fail. It is the result of research that examined the lived experiences of black college men, who had achieved successful collegiate transition. Some were in the first phase of transition, while others were further along in the middle or the end in pursuit of their degrees.

Like all of humanity, although these young men had faced a plethora of obstacles and challenges in college and in life (historical discrimination, marginalization, and disenfranchisement, whether economically, educationally, socially, etc.), yet they literally "walked on water" and were able to bounce back from setbacks and rise above the pitfalls that traditionally cause young men of color to fail in higher education. What these young men taught me, and will teach the world, is that they discovered their inherent power to succeed in higher education, and in

2

life, by accessing their "Burden of Hope ". A burden of hope is the power to succeed against many odds and persist in the face of statistics that were stacked against them, because doing so makes a better life for those who they love and who are mutually vested in their success.

Through their burden of hope, their voices will be heard and their stories will hopefully enlighten and provide the insight needed to deal with young men of color in a balanced methodology. This area acknowledges their humanomics: in terms of not just the traditional emphasis on *supply*, in regards to what need deficiencies they have, but also an emphasis on *demand*, in regards to what personal assets they possess, such as desire, motivation, skills, abilities, and a willingness to systematic use their inherent power and inherent resilience to systematically respond to adversity and challenges with a greater resilience or hustle, in order to make their transition in college and in life successful.

When tomorrow becomes today, we are in a moment of decision called "the urgency of now." Dr. Martin Luther King's words are an accurate description of the moment of decision that young men of color and all of humanity find themselves in: it is time to abandon "randomnimity" and haphazardness in responding to life's challenges and obstacles by embracing a systematic protocol, such as the Bumblebee and Inherent Power and Resilience Paradigm, and no longer be at the mercy of emotions that fuel desire, but not successful results. The "urgency of now" is a time to act responsibly, accountably, and decisively by responding to adversity, whether real or perceived in a well thought-out, resilient protocol, where a systematic demand is placed on personal assets of inherent power and inherent resilience. Since the plight of black and young men of color directly threatens their survival, they must begin to look within themselves for the solution to the ever-increasing marginalization that characterize their journey in our twenty-first Century world. Not only does this systemic approach to responding to adversity work for young men of color, it works for all people, especially those whose humanity attracts formidable opposition to their survival and success in life.

Bumblebees indeed can fly: not because natural law says that they can, not because their issues say they can, not because society says that they can, but because their decision to be resilient and to fly overrides every reason why they shouldn't be able to fly! The same ability in the bumblebee to do what it was created to do is also in all of humanity, including young men of color. It is called inherent power!

Because America needs all young men, including those of color, to mature and develop into adult men who can assume their responsibilities as good husbands, as well as strong and nurturing fathers, the announcement and launch of President Barak Obama's initiative to salvage the lives and potential of young men of color brought tears to my eyes. Future generations are in the seed of these young men; therefore, if they are marginalized and disenfranchised from their own potential, that automatically marginalize the future generations that come from their loins. Human capital is too precious to be squandered. All people, including young men of color, are answers to the cries and needs of all of humanity, as well as the survival of the world.

Developing Resilience and Inherent Power -Strength educational and social paradigms, as opposed to the deficit- based models that emphasize deficiencies and ignore personal assets and resources by acknowledging abilities, skills, motivation and desire of all people, including Young Men of Color, is crucial. Thus, learning to acknowledge and deploy their personal, Inherent Power and Inherent Resiliency is the only way left for the survival and success of all of humanity. Consider the statistics according to the U.S. Census Bureau: 41 percent of all US children are born to unmarried mothers. The implications are staggering: 35.7 percent Caucasian children, 68.5 percent Native American and Alaskan children, and 72.3 percent in African American children are born in homes without fathers. Because the dismal plight of young men of color is directly associated with their experiences of fatherlessness early in life, it must be addressed in any serious attempts to bring about meaningful improvement. It is important to understand that fatherlessness has reached epidemic proportions that threaten to further marginalize future young men and women who grow up in homes without a father.

Fatherlessness influence and impact several other phenomenon that have become serious human health and human rights concerns. Children without fathers in the home are five times more likely to live in poverty than those raised by two married parents. Nearly one third of single female-led households live in poverty, versus 16.9% of single male-led households and only 5.8% of two-parent married homes. Women are remarkable, resilient, and worthy of much praise for all they do. But single-parent homes have not always been the norm. According to the U.S. Census Bureau, 78% of all African American households were led by two-parent married couples in the 1950s as opposed 28.7% today.

The breakdown of the family, especially in the lives of young men of color, is seriously tied to their dismal achievement, lack of success, and overall plight in America. The CDC has revealed that infant mortality among children of unmarried women increases 78% compared to children in homes with two married parents. Youth, including young men of color who are without fathers in their homes, are twice as likely to drop out of school. They are also at much higher risk of low achievement, crime, incarceration, and drug trafficking, as well as substance abuse, teenage pregnancy, and the perpetuation of historical cycles of generational poverty. America must understand that the very future of our nation and its people is tied to the stabilization of the crisis concerning young men of color.

A major part of any conversation concerning young men of color must include an awareness of their God-given inherent power and personal resilience to succeed and achieve through embracing their burden of hope, which is fueled by their desire to make life better for those whose lives are vested in them and their success. When this happens, young men of color will find the inner strength to assume their place of accountability and responsibility so that the children who enter the world through their loins will be immunized against the lethal effects of marginalized living.

The ever-increasing escalation of marginalization, profiling, crime, and violence among and against young men of color can be capped and eventually defused. It is a complex issue that cannot be trivialized; however, it is a human issue and therefore it can be confronted and reduced by necessary information and resolve at various levels of accountability and responsibility. A major part of any conversation in this regard must include acknowledging the fact that the same inherent power in bumblebees that lets them fly is also in black and other young men of color. If they can learn how to access it and apply it, their plight which looks as though it is impossible to solve will be overcome. After all, the Holy Scriptures say in Ephesians 3:20: "Now unto Him that is able to do exceedingly and abundantly above and beyond all that we may ask or think according to the power that works in us" (NKJV). If God placed inherent power in bumblebees, He also placed it in all of humanity, including young men of color!

Bumblebees Can Fly: Inherent Power and Inherent Resiliency

Bumblebees fly because the personal inherent power and personal inherent resilience in them are greater than the laws of aerodynamics and other physical laws that work against them. Like Young Men of Color and the rest of humanity, when adversity and challenges are viewed through the lens of the personal assets of inherent power and resiliency, it changes personal perception from a paradigm of victimization to one of empowerment.

CHAPTER TWO

THE URGENCY OF NOW: NEED FOR PERSONAL POLICY TO BRING ABOUT PERSONAL RESILIENCE:

We are now faced with the fact with the fact
That tomorrow is today. We are confronted with the
fierce urgency of now. This is no time for apathy
or complacency. This is a time for vigorous and
positive action.
-Dr. Martin Luther King, Jr.

Pressure cannot produce benefit where there is no personal protocol or personal policy in place to create a systematic process for bringing about a systematic response to challenges and adversity, resulting in greater resiliency and success.

Resilience: Personal Power and Personal Strength that resides in the person. Resilience is the ability to bounce back, rebound, and come back from adversity, stronger, healthier, and better than before the opposition or challenge; however, resilience works best when it is the result of a personal policy that is not haphazard or random in response to various adverse events.

When tomorrow becomes today, we find ourselves in a moment of decision that Dr. Martin Luther King, Jr. referred to as "the urgency of now." Young black and brown men are disproportionately affected by the inhumane effects of marginalization in several ways, such as K–12 school dropout rates, dismal rates of transition, retention, and persistence in postsecondary education, disproportionate rates of incarceration, and higher rates of death inflicted through violence.

Resilience in the Bumblebee is argued in regards to the person-centric paradigm for finally stopping the endless bleeding of Young Men of Color. Despite its heavy and large body, the bumblebee is able to fly-defying the Law of Aerodynamics. The bumblebee flies because its' Inherent Power and Inherent Resilience, due to intentional adversity that it faces as a way of life, is greater than its challenges, aerodynamics and gravity, included.

Of all the nations in the world, America was founded as a place where theoretically all the disenchanted and discouraged could enter better lives through America's front door of personal inherent power and personal inherent resilience in order to participate in the American dream, where all could tap into the power within to dream, work hard, and work smart to live their best life and realize their full potential. However, the history of America demonstrates that until they learned to access their inherent power from within themselves through sheer determination, faith, and hard work, America's front door was initially closed to certain people, like the Irish, Italians, Polish, Native Americans, Hispanics, and certainly those of African ancestry.

The history of America is littered with example upon example of people of African descent being relegated to America's "back door," which is a euphemism for looking everywhere but within themselves for affirmation and empowerment to reach their full potential as contributing members of American democracy and authorized benefactors of the American dream. Since slavery, and up to and including this present time, people of color have not been given access to the front door of the American dream.

African American athletes and artists for the most part have discovered America's front door by utilizing the inherent power within them in order to reach their dreams. Minorities have yet to apply the same principle in achieving success in academics and other areas of life through a decision to tap into their inherent power to fulfill their Burden of Hope in order to make life better for themselves and those who are vested in their success and survival.

Entering through the "back door" is a metaphor for the power that perceptions of marginalization have that deny young men of color their inalienable right to use their God-given inherent power to unlock their potential in order to create a better life for themselves and to realize their Burden of Hope in order to secure better lives for those with whom they share emotional vesting. When young black and brown men perceive that they have been denied access to fulfill their Burden of Hope, through alienation from their potential and inherent power, they will attempt to fulfill their Burden of Hope through the "back door" or other means than their own inherent power to succeed, achieve, and realize their God-given potential. When there is no access to being empowered from within, in desperation and poor choices, they will attempt to access life through the back door, which manifests as crime, violence, illegal drug use and sale, as well as other forms of deviant behavior.

Inherent power/ resilience is defined as an authority possessed without it being derived from another. It is a right, ability or faculty of doing something, without receiving that right, ability or faculty from another. Inherent power is not a luxury given to some people, it is part of every individual's humanity; one of the "Inalienable rights, such as life, liberty, and the pursuit of happiness." The Burden of Hope is defined as the desire to use one's Inherent power to protect, provide for, and positively affect the lives of others who one believes are dependent on him or her, or emotionally vested in his or her success and survival.

Historical economic, racial, gender, and ethnic disparities have the power to bring about perceptions of marginalization not only in black and brown men, but also in other groups who have suffered historical disparities that inhibit them from experiencing the depths of the American dream. Young black and brown men are exceptionally vulnerable to the lethal effects of being marginalized and disenfranchised, which deny them their right to use their inherent power to unlock their Burden of Hope which research indicates has the power to cause them to change their deviant behavior and improve their lives.

It goes without saying that eradicating marginalization and its effects calls for a collaborative effort, which cuts across a plethora of national, state, local, community, and individual levels. Every young man of color, as well as other powerbrokers, must share responsibility for confrontation and making quality decisions to address marginalization in its various forms, so that young men of color can overcome the effects of being alienated from their inherent power and being denied access to their Burden of Hope.

Research reveals that for young men of color, their individual Burden of Hope gives them the power not only to improve their own lives, but also to secure better lives for those with whom they share emotional vesting in regards to mutual survival and success.

"My Brother's Keeper" initiative is intended to bolster the lives of young minority men, seeking to use the power of the presidency to help a group of Americans whose lives are disproportionately affected by poverty and prison. It is a collaborative initiative that hopes to bring foundations and companies together to test a range of strategies to support such young men, taking steps to keep them in school and out of the criminal justice system. The effort will seek "to make sure that every young man of color who is willing to work hard and lift himself up has an opportunity to get ahead and reach his full potential."

America is to be congratulated for officially acknowledging that young men of color are experiencing a crisis that demands the immediate attention and efforts of not only government at every level, but also from families, churches, educational institutions, community organizations, and most of all the young men of color themselves. The latter is the primary focus for this book which is written to call attention to an overlooked and underutilized strategy for helping to end the struggle of young men of color. That is to teach them to use their inherent power to end the bleeding that has categorized them as an endangered species.

Bumblebees Can Fly: Inherent Power and Inherent Resiliency

Like the bumblebee, the response to adversity, challenges, failure, and setbacks need to be a decisive decision that is increasingly proactive and resilient. If bumblebees can fly and they have been doing so for eons, despite the law of aerodynamics that says that they shouldn't be able to so; then, all of humanity, including young men of color **can use their personal inherent power and personal inherent resiliency, in the face of adversity, failure, and setbacks to bounce back from every setback in life!**

CHAPTER THREE

BUT FOR GRACE. . .
Resilient Grace in Response to Real or Perceived Adversity

But remember me when it goes well for you, and
show me kindness. Make mention of me to Pharaoh
and bring me out of this prison. (Gen 39:14)

Resilience in the Bumblebee is argued in regards to the person-centric paradigm for finally stopping the endless of bleeding of Young Men of Color. Despite its heavy and large body, the bumblebee is able to fly-defying the Law of Aerodynamics. The bumblebee flies because its' Inherent Power and Inherent Resilience, due to intentional adversity that it faces as a way of life, is greater than its challenges, aerodynamics and gravity, included.

In Bumblebees Can Fly, Dr. Dowdell-Underwood argues that like the bumblebee, all marginalized, disenfranchised and historically discriminated people must understand that adversity, Biblically and scientifically, is present in order to bring about greater resilience in order to intentionally succeed where failure would be the normal outcome or default result.. It is through greater awareness of resources and personal assets, that empower humanity, including Young Men of Color to use their personal Inherent Power and Inherent Resiliency to overcome the lethal effects of the various types of adversity that they attract in life, empowering them to maximize their personal potential. This will effectively result in ending the continued societal loss that results when brilliant Young Men and Young Women of Color, and other disenfranchised and, or marginalized people fail to constructively deploy their potential and live a healthy life.

Young men of color continue to be marginalized by being disproportionately incarcerated, policed, unemployed, and victimized by violence and miseducation. The incarceration rates disproportionately impact men of color: one in every fifteen African American men and one in every thirty-six Hispanic men are incarcerated in comparison to one in every 106 white men. According to the Bureau of Justice Statistics, one in three black men can expect to go to prison in their lifetime. Individuals of color have a disproportionate number of encounters with law enforcement, indicating that racial profiling continues to be a problem. A report by the Department of Justice found that blacks and Hispanics were approximately three times more likely to be searched during a traffic stop than white motorists. African Americans were twice as likely to be arrested and almost four times as likely to experience the use of force during encounters with the police (Kirby, 2012). Marginalization begins early in the lives of young men of color. In fact, students of color face harsher punishments in school than their white peers, leading to a higher number of youth of color incarcerated.

Black and Hispanic students represent more than 70 percent of those involved in school-related arrests or referrals to law enforcement. Currently, African Americans make up two-fifths and Hispanics one-fifth of confined youth. According to recent data by the Department of Education, African American students are arrested far more often than their white classmates. The data showed that 96,000 students were arrested and 242,000 referred to law enforcement by schools during the 2009–10 school year. Of those students, black and Hispanic students made up more than 70 percent of arrested or referred students. Harsh school punishments, from suspensions to arrests, have led to high numbers of youth of color coming into contact with the juvenile justice system and at an earlier age.

The ability to find gainful employment is a human dignity that is crucial in building and developing character and work ethic. The number of young men of color without jobs has climbed relentlessly, with only a slight pause during the economic peak of the late 1990's. In 2000, 65 percent of black male high school dropouts in their twenties were either unemployed, unable to find a job, not looking for a job, or incarcerated. By 2004, those numbers had climbed to 72 percent, compared with 34 percent of white and 19 percent of Hispanic dropouts. The impact of marginalization and discrimination among young men of color, especially black men, is seen in the fact that when high school graduates were included in the sampling, half of black men in their twenties were jobless in 2004, up from 46 percent in 2000 (Eckholm, 2006).

Incarceration rates climbed in the 1990's and reached historic proportions in the past few years. In 1995, 16 percent of black men in their twenties who did not attend college were in jail or prison; by 2004, 21 percent were incarcerated. By their mid-thirties, 6 in 10 black men who had dropped out of school had spent time in prison. In the inner cities, more than half of all black men do not finish high school (Eckholm, 2006). .

Resilience: Personal Power and Personal Strength that resides in the person. Resilience is the ability to bounce back, rebound, and come back from adversity, stronger, healthier, and better than before the opposition or challenge; however, resilience works best when it is the result of a personal policy that is not haphazard or random in response to various adverse events. As dismal as these statistics are, there are countless young men of color who have discovered the inner fortitude to overcome the odds stacked against them and live productive lives. It is crucial to discover the reasons why these young men of color have succeeded so that a greater number can also improve their lot in life. This book is a call to deal with young men of color by providing redemptive environments that empower, rather than further marginalize, the potential and inherent power in them. The heart of the message of inherent power is revealed through the strength of establishing environments that are rich in grace, high expectations, accountability, and forgiveness. Those environments, whether verbal, intellectual, social, emotional, or physical, empower young men of color to look within themselves for the strength to achieve and succeed not only in school but also in life.

Historical experiences with racism, disenfranchisement, and marginalization lose the power to lock young men of color in cycles of hopelessness, poor choices, failure, and deviant behavior when they have families, teachers, administrators, counselors, mentors, churches, and community organizations that refuse to lose sight of the potential in each of these young men. Inherent power is not just in some people; it is in all people. It is the common denominator in human achievement and rehabilitation. inherent power holds the promise of empowering young men of color to assume responsibility for the contour and context of their lives; however, the true depths of inherent power and human potential can only surface when redemptive environments such as identified in this book are allowed to continually resuscitate hope through reoccurring redemptive responses that refuse to write these young men off or to give up on them.

This book is a compilation of over forty years in the trenches, coaching human potential for the purposes of success and achievement in adults and children alike. It is written to codify those practices good teachers and coaches of human learning and growth do automatically. By putting a face to these practices, it is hoped that millions of children and adults will be positively impacted and experience an explosion in human potential.

In the fast-paced twenty-first century life, it is customary to simply dismiss those who don't learn as people who can't learn, without ever taking the time to do some soul-searching to find out why they haven't learned. Educational psychology labels many young men of color, especially young black men, as learning disabled, and as a result takes them off of educational life support, leaving their potential frozen in the fires of frustration. The result is an angry and confused soul!

This book is written to attend to this group of neglected humanity, by reconnecting them with their destinies and exposing the number one culprit in learning enablement—the five environments in which humanity grows and develops. These environments are the power brokers whose dynamic operation decides the extent to which the individual grows, learns, and achieves. Many people struggle for years with things that present stumbling blocks to achievement because they don't understand that personality has the ability to change as the environment changes. Significant people who have the ability to shape the environments that paint the portrait of self on the canvas of the soul are parents, siblings, teachers, principals, and role models, such as athletes or those of the entertainment media, as well as the individual's peer group. For adults, their spouses, pastors, and supervisors are also part of this class.

The environment that nurtures resiliency is constructed by those humanity, in particular young men of color, perceive are of great value and importance to them. These environments are potential and personal friendly. Personal inherent power and resiliency are activated when their burden of hope is unlocked through their desire to achieve and overcome because it positively affects those who they believe are vested in their success and survival. The significance assigned connotes the ability to transfer value. This is serious because if that individual or child perceives someone as having value, then consequential opinion and attitudes are magnified and carry great weight in regard to the shaping of his or her concept of self.

Five resiliency environments, which together form the total picture of the self of young men of color, are formed by the attitudes and opinions of those considered to be significant to them. They can shape the reflection of God on that person's heart or change the reflection that is already there, as well as enforce or even abort what has already been encoded in the heart and mind concerning perceived potential and ability. The Word of God says that as a man thinks in his heart so is he. The psyche or will of the individual is influenced by several environments or messages that have influenced and shaped the reflection of self that is resident in the heart or mind of every man or woman.

Bumblebees Can Fly:
Inherent Power and Inherent Resiliency

In Bumblebees Can Fly, Dr. Dowdell-Underwood argues that like the bumblebee, all marginalized, disenfranchised and historically discriminated people must understand that adversity, Biblically and scientifically, is present in order to bring about greater resilience in order to intentionally succeed where failure would be the normal outcome or default result.. It is through greater awareness of resources and personal assets, that empower humanity, including Young Men of Color to use their personal Inherent Power and Inherent Resiliency to overcome the lethal effects of the various types of adversity that they attract in life, empowering them to maximize their personal potential. This will effectively result in ending the continued societal loss that results when brilliant Young Men and Young Women of Color, and other disenfranchised and, or marginalized people fail to constructively deploy their potential and live a healthy life.

CHAPTER FOUR

THE NEED FOR ENVIRONMENTS THAT NURTURE PERSONAL RESILIENCE

I t is a well-documented fact that even the most-able and most-gifted people, whether children or adults, tend to adopt the expectations of the environment that they are a part of, whether it happens to be instructional or social, etc.,. Therefore, it is crucial that those who like the bumblebees, face formidable, life- adversity, adopt a systemic policy and protocol to counter the lethal effects of adversity by their inherent power and inherent resiliency instead of the challenges that prey on their potential and survival. Akin to resilience, redemptive is defined as the purchase back of something that had been lost. Resilience: Personal Power and Personal Strength that resides in the person. Resilience is the ability to bounce back, rebound, and come back from adversity, stronger, healthier, and better than before the opposition or challenge; however, resilience works best when it is the result of a personal policy that is not haphazard or random in response to various adverse events. Besides its traditional use as one's surroundings, *environment* is defined as the social and cultural forces that shape the life of a person or a population. Thus in this book *redemptive environments* are defined as those social and cultural forces that have the ability to cause young men of color to reclaim their inherent power and human potential, and thus recapture and reshape their own lives. Environment is crucial, since bumblebees never attempt to fly in climates that are not conducive for their emergence.

The common denominator in all human achievement and rehabilitation is the ability to discover and access the inherent power, resilience, and potential within every individual. That is the case in point in regards to young men of color. By all measurements, these young men lag behind all other groups. This book argues that the reason for their dismal condition is due in large part to them being not only alienated from awareness of and access to their inherent power, but also them being alienated from the redemptive environments that are needed in order to cause inherent power and potential to surface.

The acknowledgement of resilience in disenfranchised and marginalized people has been borne out by research that endeavored to discuss the scientific definition, conceptualization and measurement of resilience (American Psychological Association Task Force on Resilience and Strength in Black Children and Adolescents, 2008; Resnick, 2000).

One area of consensus that research has revealed is that resilience exists in the context of real or perceived adversity (Fergus & Zimmerman, 2005; Luthar, Cicchetti and Becker, 2000; Masten, 2001, Spencer, Harpalani, Cassidy, Jacobs, Donde, Goss et al., 2006).

Resilient environments are able to release messages of empowerment that shape and cultivate beliefs regarding young men of color ability to dream big, work hard, and produce desired levels of performance and achievement. These environments have the power to change these young men's perceptions concerning how they feel, think, and see their future, even to the point of causing them to summon the self-efficacy (inherent power) to overcome detrimental behavior (Bandura, 1993). Inherent power is relegated to the redemptive environments that cultivate belief systems that empower rather than denigrate young men of color. Where young men of color have access to redemptive environments, they are able to overcome depression, anger, anxiety, and perceived helplessness. In redemptive environments, these lost young men of America discover the power to make quality choices that positively impact their achievement and their overall lives.

Self–efficacy or the use of one's inherent power refers to one's beliefs regarding perceived ability to produce desired levels of performance affecting one's life. It can have positive impact concerning how young men of color feel, think, and motivate themselves to behave (Bandura,

1993). Much of the anger experienced by young men of color is the result of their having low self-efficacy because they are alienated from their inherent power, which in turn can be associated with depression, anxiety, and helplessness. When young men of color have access to redemptive environments, they will be less prone to making poor decisions, since the quality of decision making, as well as academic achievement, are negatively affected by perceptions of low self-efficacy or awareness of one's inherent power. People in general, as well as young men of color who struggle with low self-efficacy, tend to harbor self-doubt and are timid and hesitant to explore new possibilities, opportunities, or ideas.

On the other hand, young men of color who are able to defy the odds that are stacked against them, do so in part because they have access to redemptive environments that developed healthy inherent power and high self-efficacy, causing them to not be afraid of tend to perform challenging tasks. People in general, and young men of color in particular, who have access to redemptive environments and their inherent power are able to set high goals for their lives and remain focused until these goals are achieved.

Self-efficacious people are prone to exploring new environments or creating alternative ones. Should they encounter setbacks, they are prone to overcome challenges easier than their less-efficacious counterparts who by virtue being alienated from needed redemptive environments are also alienated from their inherent power.

The importance of self-efficacy is illustrated in the old Chinese proverb: "Give a man a fish and he will eat for a day; teach a man to fish and he can feed himself for a lifetime." This idea is crucial in education's journey toward developing competency in all of the world's children (Jacoby & Associates, 1996). In education, the struggle to meet mandated proficiency, it continues to ignore the most important variable in the learning equation—namely the learner. If serious progress is to be realized by 2014, empowering students through self-efficacy and peer intellectual engagement must be taken more seriously.

Research demonstrates a strong relationship exists between student beliefs and their education, and their subsequent ability to achieve (Pajores,1996). Billie Holiday's lyrics are applicable in this regard: "Mama may have, papa may have, but God bless the child that's got his own" (Holiday, 1939). If education is to realize greater student achievement among all students, including young men of color, regardless of socioeconomic status, there needs to be a shift in emphasis from controlling students and their learning to one of empowering students and teachers to facilitate greater learning (Martin & MacNeil, 2007).

The education of all children, regardless of race or socioeconomic status, has placed public school education under the microscope of public scrutiny. This is borne out by federal initiatives such as No Child Left Behind Act (No Child Left Behind, 2002). As a result of this emphasis, the United States government is requiring the states to demonstrate greater educational accountability in regards to the achievement of all students at the state and individual local school corporation levels. An examination of research, such as that by Charles Sykes reveals that a dumbing-down of academic expectations for poor and minority students translates into a difference in achievement in comparison with other groups (Sykes, 1995). He goes on to say that these students are often treated as if they cannot handle the rigor of learning. Attitudes such as this indicate a problem with teacher efficacy in regards to perceived beliefs not only about these children's ability to learn but also the teachers' ability to instruct them (Edmonds, 1979).

Research conducted by Moran and Hoy implies that important educational outcomes have been proven to be powerfully related to teacher efficacy, such as teachers' persistence, enthusiasm, commitment and instructional behavior, and that these are related to student outcomes, such as achievement, motivation, and self-efficacy beliefs (Moran, 2001, pp. 783–805). The researchers noted that it is difficult to measure teacher efficacy. Teacher self-efficacy refers to the level at which a teacher feels capable of supporting students' learning. Collective teacher efficacy is a specific belief in the capacity of teachers as a whole to have a positive effect on students (Goddard, 2002). Collective teacher differs from individual teacher efficacy in that collective efficacy refers to the effective abilities of all teachers, whereas individual teacher self-efficacy refers to beliefs about one teacher's abilities. While both are related, they are uniquely different (Gray & Ross, 2006).

The American public wants to see meaningful results and outcomes. In other words, American education is expected to deliver a well-educated populace, without excuses or equivocation (Manna, 2006). Isaacs (2003) stated accountability is used to answer the questions that concern what difference individuals or their programs have made to students, families, teachers, schools, and districts (p. 288). It follows that the greatest difference will be made in the education of students who have been empowered through self-efficacy and peer intellectual engagement to positively affect their own academic success (McNeil & Hood, 2002). Perceived self-efficacy influences teacher persistence as well as student learning (Moran, M., A.W. & Hoy, 1998).

In the same way,

Bandura reports that students' perceptions of their self-efficacy to regulate their own learning and to master academic tasks determine their aspirations, level of motivation, and academic accomplishments (Bandura, 1993). He further asserts that teachers' beliefs in their personal efficacy to motivate and promote learning affect the types of learning environments they create and the level of academic progress their students achieve. His research further revealed that student body characteristics influence school-level achievement more strongly by altering faculties' beliefs in their collective efficacy than through direct affects on school achievement. In other words, increased student achievement yields greater collective efficacy among school faculty (Goddard, Hoy & Hoy, 2004).

Much of student achievement is the result of healthy relationships of trust between the teacher and the student, as well as the teacher and leadership (Bryk & Schneider, 2000). Relationships are crucial in strengthening teacher and student efficacy in the instructional program (R. Gore, 2007). This is borne out by research, including the findings of S. Gruenert and E. Hampton, that indicates that the erosion of trust between student and teacher manifests itself in many ways, including a diminishing of academic achievement (Hampton & Gruenert, 2008). Teacher efficacy has the power to influence student efficacy as well as student achievement. Conversely, student achievement has the power to influence greater teacher efficacy and a higher quality of instruction (Bandura, 1993).

In addition to student and teacher efficacy, intellectual or cognitive engagement is an important construct to examine in regards to student achievement. Although there are many motivational constructs, self-efficacy is one that is key to promoting student engagement and learning. Self-efficacy facilitates behavior, cognition, and motivational engagement in the instructional process (Linnenbrink & Pintrich, 2003). Research conducted by Mary Ainley finds that motivation and cognitive engagement are essential for effective learning.

Motivation is essential. One common perspective in research on student motivation is to identify student qualities that are conducive to intellectual engagement in the instructional process (Ainley, paper presented in 2004).

Bandura's theory on self-efficacy states that a student's ability to learn new skills and information is influenced by the learner's sense of self-efficacy. He adds that unlike self-esteem, self-efficacy can differ greatly from one subject or performance area to another. For example, Bandera says that someone may have high self-efficacy in art but low self-efficacy concerning science.

According to Bandura, the two most powerful sources of self-efficacy are the learner's previous experiences with similar tasks and the learner's observations. He further notes that persuasion and verbal cueing and support, along with the learner's perceptions also contribute to self-efficacy (Bandura, 1969). Bandura's findings reveal that self-efficacy strengthens cognitive engagement, while Schunk's (1994) research reveals that the learner's belief that he or she is making progress enhances self-efficacy (Schunk, 1994).

Bumblebees Can Fly:
Inherent Power and Inherent Resiliency

Consistently, research points out that despite generational poverty or the absence of desired family support, Young Men of Color and others who have faced great challenges and adversity, can achieve in academics and succeed in life if their awareness of personal inherent power and personal inherent resiliency are greater than perceptions of failure, setbacks, marginalization, disenfranchisement, and victimization.

CHAPTER FIVE

ENGAGING INHERENT POWER, INHERENT RESILIENCY, EDUCATION IN ORDER TO OVERCOME LIFE CHALLENGES

If young men of color learn to use their inherent power and inherent resiliency by taking responsibility for their own success in life, challenges of marginalization, discrimination, adversity, and poverty become mere obstacles that can be overcome.

R esilience: Personal Power and Personal Strength that resides in the person. Resilience is the ability to bounce back, rebound, and come back from adversity, stronger, healthier, and better than before the opposition or challenge; however, resilience works best when it is the result of a personal policy that is not haphazard or random in response to various adverse events. Poor choices, such as gang involvement, crime, violence, or other deviant behavior, are not an inherent part of young men of color, and as history shows us, these things can be overcome not only by the assistance that is given to them but even more by the inherent power and inherent resiliency that all people, including young men of color, possess.

The acknowledgement of resilience in disenfranchised and marginalized people has been borne out by research that endeavored to discuss the definition, conceptualization and measurement of resilience (American Psychological Association Task Force on Resilience and Strength in Black Children and Adolescents, 2008; Resnick, 2000).

One area of agreement that research has revealed is that resilience exists in the framework of where adversity is either real or perceived (Fergus & Zimmerman, 2005; Luthar, Cicchetti and Becker, 2000; Masten, 2001, Spencer, Harpalani, Cassidy, Jacobs, Donde, Goss et al., 2006).

To a large extent, adversity has been defined as specific experiences and describable events (e.g., divorce) (Sandler, Wolchik, Davis, Haine, Ayers, 2003) but some include chronic adversity such as that associated with poverty (Cauce, Stewart, Rodriguez, Cochran, Ginzler, 2003). Some use terms like "invincible" or "walking on water" to describe resilience as a fixed trait (Rutter, 1985; Werner and Smith, 1989). Resilience-based strategies can help to reduce health risk behaviors by building on assets in the individual, family and community (Davies, Thind, Chandler and Tucker, 2011).

History confirms that where perceptions of marginalization, discrimination, and disenfranchisement exist, young men, whether Italian Americans, Irish Americans, African Americans, Hispanic Americans, Asian Americans, or others. who are disenfranchised from using their inherent power and cannot fulfill their desire and need to achieve through traditional or accepted social and economic structures, will find alternative means by which to live.

Specifically, these groups of people are marginalized by society on the basis of their race, nationality, and/or economic background. This marginalization translates into mischaracterization (branding), disparate treatment, hostility, and social exclusion toward these groups. As a result, these groups self-protect and create their own opportunities for success, which often manifests as dysfunctional living. However, through better knowledge, better choices, and greater accountability for their own success, these obstacles can be overcome.

Dr. Dowdell-Underwood argues that like the bumblebee, all marginalized, disenfranchised and historically discriminated people can also use their personal Inherent Power and Inherent Resiliency to overcome the lethal effect of marginalization and maximize their human potential. This will effectively result in ending the continued societal loss that results when brilliant Young Men and Young Women of Color, and other disenfranchised and, or marginalized people fail to constructively deploy their potential and live a healthy life.

Research consistently points out that education is a crucial component in overcoming not only the perception of marginalization but also its various effects, such as poverty, crime, violence, and incarceration. For that reason, this conceptual framework and overview emphasizes practical recommendations to reduce educational marginalization, through young men of color using their inherent power. In learning to take responsibility for the contour and context of their lives, young men of color will discover the power to be better served by the American Dream and as with those once-disenfranchise groups of young men before them, they, too, will begin to make the contributions that America needs in order to remain healthy and strong.

Although, schools must establish high expectations for all students— and provide the support necessary to achieve these expectations. It is even more important for young men of color to have high expectations for themselves. As powerful as experiences of historical discrimination, marginalization, and disenfranchisement are, the inherent power within young men of color can overcome the effects of these challenges when they are met with a resolve to believe in their potential and expect more out of themselves in life.

The acknowledgement of resilience in disenfranchised and marginalized people has been borne out by research that endeavored to discuss the scientific definition, conceptualization and measurement of resilience (American Psychological Association Task Force on Resilience and Strength in Black Children and Adolescents, 2008; Resnick, 2000).

One area of consensus that research has revealed is that resilience exists in the context of real or perceived adversity (Fergus & Zimmerman, 2005; Luthar, Cicchetti and Becker, 2000; Masten, 2001, Spencer, Harpalani, Cassidy, Jacobs, Donde, Goss et al., 2006).

Research consistently confirms that high expectations are a crucial component in student achievement and success. (Rutter, 1979; Edmonds, 1979; Slavin, 1979). Inherent power is the result of an individual possessing the motivation within that unlocks the power to do what needs to be done in order to achieve a desired result. Perception orders motivation, which in turn orders behavior. It must be remembered that violence, crime, substance abuse, and drug use and sales are behaviors, but so are achievement and success; therefore, they can be strengthened, modified, or if need be, even eradicated by better knowledge, resolve, and a change of perception. Inherent power in teachers' decisions to teach and students' decisions to learn are also behaviors; they are subject to internal and external climate issues such as expectations, attitude and expectation, which have the power to overcome perceptions and effects of marginalization.

The continual exit of young men of color, especially those of African American descent, from secondary institutions without a high school diploma is more than an educational issue; it is a human rights issue as well. For this reason, there must be a concerted initiative at every level of the educational paradigm that calls for reform that among other things, seeks to establish climates or belief systems of high expectations for all students, but especially for young men of color.

It must be more than simply a local emphasis based on teacher perceptions; it must be part of the competency and proficiency mandate at every level of the educational continuum. Where educational institutions create cultures that have a zero tolerance for the marginalization of any student or group, through evidence-based teaching and commitment to the eradication of practices of instructional marginalization through corporate instructional excellence and student achievement, then the students in those schools, including young men of color, will have greater rates of achievement and success.

Research consistently demonstrates a crucial relationship between climate issues, such as instructional expectations, and student achievement, unemployment, crime, and violence among young men of color. Low-achieving students are less likely to be called upon, and if they are, they are likely to be asked the easier questions that don't serve to challenge their cognitive development. Students have a way of internalizing educational climate and as a result often are less motivated to learn and achieve (Accel team, 2006).

Instructional expectations must become more systematic in order to bring about systematic achievement and competency among high- and low-performing students, such as a disproportionate number of young men of color. For too long personal experiences and preference have dictated instructional practices in education; the price that has been paid is incompetency, steadily widening achievement gaps, escalation in crime, and the alienation of many groups, especially young men of color, from the possibility of better lives. Personal perception drives expectations in dealing with others, and in the case of education, it also drives instructional practices, which in turn, drive student achievement or non-achievement. Instructional expectations, along with all other curriculum and instructional strategies, must evolve from research and a commitment to have marginalized-free educational environments. Personal experiences and preferences can no longer decide what groups are permitted or denied educational achievement.

It is well documented that students tend to internalize the expectations of their teachers and will therefore only learn as much as the instructional climate allows them to learn; however, all students, but Young Men of Color, in particular, need to adopt an achievement model that focuses more on their internal environment of personal inherent power and inherent resilience in order to counter the effects of the external environment and its hostile forces. Because curriculum is the framework by which all instruction occurs within a school or classroom, motivational climates, external and internal, must be established that maximize student achievement and meeting of academic standards. The curriculum is more than the "what" of education; by definition it must also address the "how" that the "what" is taught and mastered. High teacher expectations are the heart of fostering climates that bring about the cultures of instructional excellence and student achievement and competence.

Climate is not a separate phenomenon from curriculum; rather, it exists to ensure that the curriculum is taught for mastery. Academic expectations are nothing more than teachers' attitudes in regards to a student's ability to learn the curriculum. Research says when those expectations are high, the student achieves; however, when those expectations are low, the student will demonstrate low academic performance. During the last decade, research on successful initiatives for youth at risk of academic failure has clearly demonstrated that high expectations—with concomitant support—is a critical factor in decreasing the number of students who drop out of school and in increasing the number of youth who go on to college (Pathways Home, 2005).

Research consistently demonstrates that the teacher, whether in attitude or methodology, is the most important factor in student achievement; therefore, teacher expectations are too important to continue to be left at the whim of the teachers' experiences; to do so produces instructional practices that are detrimental to the academic growth of many students. Serious educational reform must look at not only curriculum content but also the instructional strategies by which curriculum is attained.

Teachers may have the most altruistic intentions; however, the fact remains that they are human. Many of their life experiences unconsciously shape their attitudes and perceptions, including perceived student ability. McDYMC (Motivating Climates that Develop Achievement and Competency in Young Men of Color) exists to place teacher expectation practices in a framework of evidence-based research and no longer personal life experiences. Longitudinal studies support the McDYMC theory that teacher expectations can predict changes in student achievement and behavior beyond effects accounted for by previous achievement and motivation (Jissim, L. & Eccles, J., 1992)

Bumblebees Can Fly:
Inherent Power and Inherent Resiliency

All students, but Young Men of Color, in particular, need to adopt an achievement model that focuses more on empowering their internal environment of personal inherent power and inherent resilience in order to counter the effects of the external environment and its hostile forces that attempt to work against their achievement in education and success in life.

CHAPTER SIX

EMPLOYING RESILIENCE STRATEGIES AND PERSONAL TRANSFORMATON

Bumblebees Can Fly offers a new paradigm for positively addressing the plethora of ways that African-American boys are disproportionately and negatively impacted in America; whether, it be through educational, employment, social, judicial, inequity and disenfranchisement.

Much has been written to address the plight of Young Men of Color; however, through the analogy of the Bumblebee, Bumblebees Can Fly goes beyond merely discussing the problem, but also offers person-centric strategies for Young Men of Color to overcome the formidable challenges in life that threaten their very survival.

There is no need to beat around the bush. If the world in general and America specifically are serious about recovering the ever-increasing number of young men of color whose potential contributions to society are being lost through early death or incarceration, educational marginalization must be addressed.

Resilience is the process of facing adversity, trauma, tragedy, threats, or extreme stress and "bouncing back" successfully without becoming too negatively affected by the experience. The concept has received growing attention because of the usefulness of possessing a reasonable amount of resilience in the face of life's difficulties. After all, who among us doesn't face major stressors, in one form or another? The question is: how can we have the resilience to deal with what happens and not be destroyed emotionally in the process?

Consistently, research points out that despite generational poverty or the absence of desired family support, young men of color and others who have faced great challenges and adversity, can achieve in academics and succeed in life if their awareness of personal inherent power and personal inherent resiliency are greater than perceptions of marginalization, disenfranchisement, and victimization.

There is a need for many kinds of reform that no longer leaves personal expectations for personal performance in the realm of the external that derive from others' life experiences as opposed to person-centric and research-based instructional methodologies. To accept anything short of this is a statement of not being serious about closing the achievement gap that exists between high- and low-performing students, which will continue to deprive young men of color as well as other students of the opportunity to achieve and succeed.

True competency and achievement are the result of implementing evidence-based instructional practices. In an endeavor to help schools make instructional expectations a systematic entity as opposed to being at the mercy of personal preference and opinions, which marginalize historically discriminated groups, especially young men of color, it is the author's recommendation that five motivational climates need to be the framework from which instructor-student contact is structured and executed. These will remove the inconsistency that results in discriminatory practices that gives deference to high-performing students in most of the world's educational institutions. Although there are many climates that affect how teacher expectations are shaped and communicated to students, five have been identified in an attempt to close the achievement gap that exists between high-performing students who have benefitted more from teacher expectations than have underperforming students.

These motivational climates are verbal, intellectual, social, emotional, and physical in nature, and they exist to systematically remove the arbitrariness by which teachers communicate expectations based on perceived student ability when teaching the curriculum. Low-achieving students will no longer be ignored or paid intellectual disrespect due to corresponding low teacher expectations. Failing to address this component of curriculum delivery would certainly further widen the achievement gap that already exists between high- and low-performing students.

High teacher expectations usually translate into high student performance; this research is based on the Pygmalion Effect that essentially says that a teacher's expectations can influence or motivate student performance. Those for whom the teacher has lower expectations will generally perform less well. This concept can be summarized in four key principles:

- Teachers form certain expectations of their students.
- Teachers communicate those expectations in various ways.
- Students tend to respond to teacher expectations by adjusting their behavior to affirm such expectations.
- The result is that the original teacher expectation orders the corresponding academic achievement and competency of the student.

Schools that establish high expectations for all students and provide the support necessary to achieve these expectations have high rates of academic success (Rutter, 1979). During the last decade, research on successful programs for youth at risk of academic failure has clearly demonstrated that high expectations—with concomitant support—is a critical factor in decreasing the number of students who drop out of school and increasing the number of students who attend college (Slavin, 1979).

A convincing body of behavioral research says that climate issues, such as teacher expectations, are crucial to student achievement. In 1971, Robert Rosenthal, a professor of social psychology at Harvard University, described an experiment in which he told a group of students that he had developed a strain of super-intelligent rats that could run mazes quickly. He then passed out perfectly normal rats at random, telling half of the students that they had the new "maze-bright" rats and the other half that they got "maze-dull" rats.

The rats that were believed to be bright improved daily in running the maze. They ran faster and more accurately, whereas the "dull" rats refused to budge from the starting point 29% of the time, while the "bright" rats refused only 11% of the time. This experiment illustrates the core principles in the power of teacher expectations to order or paralyze the motivation needed by all students to learn and achieve at deeper cognitive levels (Rosenthal, 1971).

Bumblebees Can Fly:
Inherent Power and Inherent Resiliency

Like the bumblebee, all of humanity, including Young Men of Color, must never abdicate their personal power to set personal expectation to learn whatever is being taught and their personal resiliency to succeed and bounce back against all real or perceived odds.

CHAPTER SEVEN

THE TRANSFORMATIVE POWER OF RESILIENCE ENVIRONMENTS

Being Angry If Needed, But Making Sure That It Leads To A Constructive, Resilient Response!

R esilience: Personal Power and Personal Strength that resides in the person. Resilience is the ability to bounce back, rebound, and come back from adversity, stronger, healthier, and better than before the challenging event.

Bumblebees Can Fly focuses on personal strength and personal resources that every human being, including Young Men of Color possess by virtue of their humanity, despite their formidable challenges of discrimination, marginalization, and disenfranchisement in life.

In Bumblebees Can Fly, Dr. Oscar Dowdell-Underwood challenges Young Men of Color, as well as parents, educators, churches, government, policymakers, community leaders, and nonprofit organizations to expand opportunity for Young Men of Color and other marginalized people by using their Inherent Power and Personal Resiliency to adopt a SYSTEMATIC PROTOCOL by which they can effectively overcome life challenges by recognizing the strength and resilience that is a major component of the Inherent Power that all people, by virtue of their humanity, possess without needing to seek approval of others.

In light of the fact that most view resilience as a dynamic, multidimensional construct that uses mulit-directional interaction between the person and his or her environment, (Luther et al. 2000; Masten, 2001)., Dr. Dowdell-Underwood then offers strategies for developing and implementing verbal, intellectual, social, emotional, physical, and spiritual environments that nurture resilience and empower it, as opposed to ignoring its existence and its ability to cause all people, including Young Men and Young Women of Color to overcome the plethora of formidable challenges that oppose their success in education and in life.

Consistently, research points out that despite generational poverty or the absence of desired family support, young men of color and others who have faced great challenges and adversity, can achieve in academics and succeed in life if their awareness of personal inherent power and personal inherent resiliency are greater than perceptions of marginalization, disenfranchisement, and victimization.

The purpose of this section is to present a paradigm through review and documentation of the relationship between young men of color and the lethal effects of marginalization through unlocking their inherent power and utilizing their burden of hope, which has motivational influence that can create climate dynamics that reduce perceptions of marginalization and acts of violence. .

If the reform is to produce the desired achievement, the effects of climate, the motivation of students, instructional attitudes, and instructional behaviors on learning must be examined. Research points to the fact that quality student learning is closely tied to the climate dynamics that shape the nature of motivational properties that manifest in the classroom. The best curriculum cannot bring about the necessary educational achievement if issues of climate are not addressed.

For purposes of this conceptual design, four influences of motivational climate are identified: verbal, emotional, social and physical. Each will be described individually. The achievement gap between minority and poor students has nothing to do with race and poverty and everything to do with lack of appropriate climates in order to bring about the desired achievement. Motivation and climate are not separate from curriculum, but rather a necessary part of any educational initiative that exists to bring about meaningful learning.

Learning is always predicated on appropriate motivational climates that authorize teachers to instruct at higher levels of excellence and students to learn at higher levels of achievement. There is an irreversible relationship between competency and motivational climates that is necessary to unlock human abilities. The decision to learn involves motivational capacities that don't violate human dignity and self-worth. Research indicates that once formed, expectations about ourselves tend to be self-sustaining.

Neither children nor teachers are designed to be mechanistic in their instructional operations. The nature of decisions to teach and decisions to learn necessitate thought that can be modified by motivational climate dynamics. If true educational reform is to take place in the world, the impacts of motivation and climate on teacher excellence and student achievement must be seriously addressed. It is inconceivable that rational people would dare think that individuals can ever give their best effort in climates that compromise their human worth. In this regard, this conceptual framework proposes four motivational climate messages that facilitate better instruction on the part of teachers and better learning on the part of students.

Bumblebees Can Fly:
Inherent Power and Inherent Resiliency

Like the bumblebee, those who face great adversity must effectively counter it through a non-visceral, systemic, personal policy that's based on embracing and using personal, inherent power and inherent resiliency in order to maximize potential, achieve in education, and succeed in life.

CHAPTER EIGHT

THE NEED FOR RESILIENCE ENVIRONMENTS AND CURRICULUM FOR ALL HUMANITY, INCLUDING YOUNG MEN OF COLOR IN ORDER CONSTRUCTIVELY RESPOND TO ADVERSITY AND CHALLENGES IN LIFE

In light of the fact that most view resilience as a dynamic, multidimensional construct that uses mulit-directional interaction between the person and his or her environment, (Luther et al. 2000; Masten, 2001)., Dr. Dowdell-Underwood then offers strategies for developing and implementing verbal, intellectual, social, emotional, physical, and spiritual environments that nurture resilience and empower it, as opposed to ignoring its existence and its ability to cause all people, including Young Men and Young Women of Color to overcome the plethora of formidable challenges that oppose their success in education and in life.

Resilience: Personal Power and Personal Strength that resides in the person. Resilience is the ability to bounce back, rebound, and come back from adversity, stronger, healthier, and better than before the opposition or challenge; however, resilience works best when it is the result of a personal policy that is not haphazard or random in response to various adverse events.

Bumblebees Can Fly focuses on personal strength and personal resources that every human being, including Young Men of Color possess by virtue of their humanity, despite their formidable challenges of discrimination, marginalization, and disenfranchisement in life.

In Bumblebees Can Fly, Dr. Oscar Dowdell-Underwood challenges Young Men of Color, as well as parents, educators, churches, government, policymakers, community leaders, and nonprofit organizations to expand opportunity for Young Men of Color and other marginalized people by using their Inherent Power and Personal Resiliency to adopt a SYSTEMATIC PROTOCOL by which they can effectively overcome life challenges by recognizing the strength and resilience that is a major component of the Inherent Power that all people, by virtue of their humanity, possess without needing to seek approval of others.

Resilient environments have the power to transform the person, whether young men of color or others, and thereby transform life. Abby Souza (Sousa) believes that the achievement gap is linked to race, but it is an issue that few teachers, administrators, elected officials, and parents ever want to touch. Cumulative evidence indicates a cultural bias in regards to teacher expectations that negatively impacts the academic achievement of poor and minority students (Sykes, 1995). Research consistently demonstrates a crucial relationship between culture issues (such as teacher expectations) and student achievement. The theoretical basis for McDAC (Motivating Climates that Develop Achievement and Competency) is supported by research such as that by J. Eccles, J. Jissim, and others, who describe a causal relationship between a culture of high teacher expectations and high student achievement in poor and minority students (Eccles & Jissim, 1992, pp. 947–961).

Bumblebees Can Fly offers a new paradigm for positively addressing the plethora of ways that African-American boys are disproportionately and negatively impacted in America; whether, it be through educational, employment, social, judicial, inequity and disenfranchisement.

Traditional hostility in regards to the education of poor and minority children calls for the formation of countercultures in the family, schools, classrooms, and communities in America in order to see meaningful narrowing of the achievement gap. A climate of underachievement in the education of America's poor and minority children is proof of a cultural divide in regards to educational expectations. R. Weinstein asserts that social norms within families and school cultures have tremendous power to limit a child's academic growth and achievement (Weinstein, 2002). The researcher utilizes data from case histories and ethnographic work to show research that substantiates the complex and cumulative effects of low expectations, which if addressed correctly can lead to changes in schooling that give all students the opportunity to achieve.

The research of C. Sykes indicates that disadvantaged minority students are looked upon as though they could not handle rigorous academic stress; ideas such as this, if allowed to proliferate, significantly stall the advancement of minorities (Sykes, 1995). T. L. Good and J. E. Brophy's findings reveal that self-fulfilling prophecies are the most dramatic form of teacher expectation effects because they involve changes in student behavior, whether academic or disciplinary. When teachers do nothing to challenge expectations that have stalled student achievement, it further confirms a perceived inability to see student potential. To sustain current low expectations is to prevent desired improvement in student achievement (Brophy & Good, 1970, pp. 365–374).

Much of student achievement is the result of healthy relationships of trust between the teacher and the student. Research by S. Gruenert and E. Hampton indicates that the erosion of trust between student and teacher manifests itself in many ways, including a diminishing of academic achievement (Gruenert & Hampton, 2008). Differential treatment by teachers in regards to expectations signals trust inequity that will bring about achievement inequity, much of what is seen in the achievement gap between poor and minority students and their middle- and upper-class counterparts.

When underlying cultural beliefs, norms, and values regarding educational expectations for poor and minority children are systematically addressed, it would be logical to assume that subsequent achievement will follow. Research consistently reveals that schools that create cultures of high expectations for all students—and provide the support necessary to achieve these expectations—have high rates of academic success (Rutter, Maughan, Mortimore, & Outston, 1979). In commenting on the research of Rhona Weinstein, S. Nolen of the University of Washington believes that teachers must create countercultures in their classrooms that nurture academic achievement by eliminating the use of racism, classism, or other forms of bias so that there is less differentiation in opportunities to learn (Nolen). This awareness, says Nolen, will help ensure that teachers no longer disproportionately assign poor children and children of color to lower instructional groups and lower academic tracks that have fewer opportunities for enrichment.

(Brattesani, Weinstein & Marshall, 1984, pp. 236–247) have conducted research that points out the fact that students are quite aware of differential treatment in classrooms where it is pronounced. These researchers have also found that student attitudes—and particularly the attitudes of low-expectation students—are more positive in classrooms where differential treatment is low. Because differential treatment, for the most part, affects poor and minority students in negative ways, research-based teacher expectation models must be formed that neutralize or eliminate differential treatment in regards to student achievement.

There are schools in urban centers where cultures of high teacher expectations and high student achievement exist. These educational institutions must be examined in order to target motivational climates that they have in common that serve to challenge old cultural belief patterns that nurture differential treatment in regards to teacher expectations and dismal achievement in poor and minority children (Cotton, 1989). Studies conducted by S. Gruenert and E. Hampton (2008) reveal that the realm of expectations in schools involves social capital which is important in guiding goal-seeking behavior. Putnam (2000) demonstrated empirical evidence that perception in regards to social capital (supportive relationships) has a direct impact on student achievement.

Most researchers agree that culture manifests itself through climate and in and of itself can only be qualitatively measured. However, Cox, Hutchinson, King, and McAvoy (2005) assert that climate, which is the surface manifestation of culture, can be quantitatively assessed. Gruenert and Hampton (2008) conducted one of a few studies that looked beyond the family and sociological demographics to examine how other variables, such as expectations, influence the achievements of poor and minority students.

Culture is perpetuated by beliefs and perception, which orders climate and motivation. Behaviors such as achievement are the result of the climate which nurtures the invisible variable of culture (CinqMars, 2006). McDAC (Motivating Climates that Develop Achievement and Competency) exists for the purpose of monitoring the framework in which teacher expectations are expressed in the classroom, particularly in the instructional process. Longitudinal studies support the fact that teacher expectation functions as a differentiating factor in student achievement; therefore, I hypothesize that the systematic monitoring of the expression of teacher expectations can predict how students will achieve, beyond the effects accounted for by previous achievement and motivation (Eccles & Jissim, 1992). Since climate is the primary way to affect cultural beliefs, the McDAC theory can utilize motivational climates in order to protect the social capital of poor and minority children and to a large extent remove bias from further threatening academic achievement (Tauber, 1998). Tauber further asserts that teacher expectations can predict changes in student achievement and behavior. This is borne out by the evidence that many teachers, in fact, believe that they can judge ahead of time how certain students are likely, over time, to achieve and behave. Once these expectations are put in motion, they function to both predict and order low student achievement and negative behavior.

Additional research indicates that in forming expectations for students, teachers also label based on characteristics such as body build (Brylinsky & Moore, 1984, pp. 170–181). Gender, as well as race, ethnicity, name/surname, dialect, and socioeconomic levels are also characteristics on which teacher expectations are based (Tauber, 1998). Hunsberger and Cavanagh (1988, pp. 70–74) conducted research that indicates physical attractiveness of students can be an important factor in the formation of teacher expectations. Findings are clear that when it comes to a person's body build, mesomorphs, those with square, rugged shoulders, small buttocks, and muscular bodies, are "better" than both ectomorphs (those with thin, frail-looking bodies) and endomorphs (those with chubby, stout bodies with a central concentration of mass).

(Rosenthal and Jacobson (1968) identified four factors in regard that influence teacher expectation: climate, feedback, input, and output. Climate is the means by which culture (belief systems) surfaces; Tauber asserts that climate, as well as the other factors, is better controlled (monitored), if teachers are aware that they are operating in the first place. Tauber recommends that even if teachers do not really believe that a student is capable of greater achievement, they should act as if they hold high expectations for all students.

The McDAC theory can provide teachers with a methodology for consistently monitoring motivational climates that will limit the ways culture is allowed to minimize student achievement in poor and minority children. According to Rosenthal's research, climate, which is the socio-emotional mood or spirit created by the person holding the expectation, is often communicated nonverbally (e. g., smiling and nodding more often, providing greater eye contact, leaning closer to the student). Feedback provides both affective information (e.g., praise and less criticism of high-expectation students) and cognitive information (e.g., more detailed, as well as higher-quality feedback as to the correctness of higher-expectation students' responses). Input says that teachers tend to teach more to students of whom they expect more. Output, on the other hand, says that teachers tend to encourage greater responsiveness from those students of they expect more through their verbal and nonverbal behaviors (i.e., providing students with greater opportunities to seek clarification).

Tauber (1988) implies that if the four factors are monitored better in the classroom dynamics, the result will be improvement in student achievement, especially in the education of those who have traditionally be underserved by education and disenfranchised by teacher expectations. The McDAC theory, which targets five motivating climates, endeavors to predict student achievement through the monitoring of the means by which teacher expectations are communicated to children.

The first motivating climate, the positive communication of teacher expectations, calls for the monitoring of the verbal exchange from teacher to student. Brophy and Good (1970) and others have found that some teachers interact with students for whom they hold low expectations in such a way as to limit their academic development. For example, teachers give low-expectation students less time to answer during class recitations than perceived high-achieving students. Low-achieving students, on the other hand, are criticized for failure more often and more severely than high-expectation students.

In addition, research indicates that the verbal interactions between teachers and low-expectation students are less friendly (Cotton, 1989). Low-expectation students also asked less cognitively-complex questions than their high-expectation colleagues. Research also indicates that low-expectation students are given less public feedback than high-expectation students, as well as calling on low-expectation students less-frequently than high expectation students (Brookover, Beady, Flood, Schweitzer & Wisenbaker, 1979).

The second motivating climate for strengthening teacher expectations calls for the monitoring of how teachers provide clues to perceived intellectual ability in the classroom setting. Research indicates that low-expectation students are given fewer opportunities than high-expectation students to learn new information. Low-expectation students are given less exciting instruction, as well as fewer clues to elicit correct responses. The instruction of low-expectation students contains more rote drill and practice activities, which emphasize less meaning and conceptualization (Brophy & Good, 1984). Low-expectation students have less time allotted to them to answer a question in public classroom instruction. In research involving twelve first graders, teachers consistently favored high-ability over low-ability students in demanding and reinforcing quality performance.

The third motivating climate for strengthening teacher expectations of poor and minority students monitors teacher interactions with students that strengthen or weaken social capital. S. Hillman (1984) Conducted research that compared ten low-achieving schools in terms of students', teachers', and principals' achievement expectations for students and their sense of self-efficacy. Findings indicated that high-achieving schools were characterized by higher expectations and a stronger sense of self-efficacy.

The research of Gruenert and Hampton (2008) reveals that social capital does impact student achievement. Students who have a supportive social nexus will experience greater levels of achievement. A vast number of poor and minority students must be provided the social capital in schools and classrooms to bring about the achievement that will strengthen self-efficacy. R. Edmonds conducted research that discovered that teacher expectations and supportive school relationships do enhance the school attitudes of poor, inner-city children. High expectations were identified as a critical component of effective schooling (Edmonds, 1979, pp. 15–18).

The fourth motivating climate for improving teacher expectations toward poor and minority students targets the socio-emotional perceptions that are internalized by students as a result of teacher-student engagement. Brittensani, et al. (1984) and Good (1983) as well as others have conducted research on student awareness of differential treatment as a result of teacher expectations. Research indicates that student attitudes, particularly those of low-expectation students, are more positive in classrooms where differential treatment is low. Hunsberger and Cavanagh (1988) found that not only do teachers form expectations of students, but students form expectations of teachers. Low-expectation students are not only taught less cognitively complex information but also do not expect their teachers to teach them such challenging academic material as their high-achieving classmates (Marshall & Weinstein, 1985).

The fifth and final motivating climate for strengthening teacher expectation towards poor and minority students monitors the physical climate in which instruction occurs. Research (Team, 2006) reveals research that teachers communicate their expectations for students in a variety of ways, including the physical arrangement of student seating and physical distance that is kept between teacher and students. Expectations, as communicated school wide and in classrooms, can and do affect student achievement and attitudes (Cotton, 1989). The physical segregation of low-expectation from high-expectation students by ability grouping and tracking publicly subjects low-expectation students to differential treatment that limit academic achievement.

Research consistently reveals that teacher expectations and accompanying behaviors, whether verbal, intellectual, social, emotional, or physical, all have very real effects on student achievement. Education reform must seek to establish motivating climates that challenge the authority of erroneous cultural beliefs that further disenfranchise poor and minority students from their human and social capital. If culture has the power to manifest attitudes and behavior, then the inverse can occur, so that a change in climate can positively change culture and its expression (Tem, 2006). What do Russell Elementary School in Lexington, Kentucky; Expo for Excellence Elementary in Saint Paul, Minnesota; Sky View Junior High School in Bethel, Washington; Key Learning Community in Indianapolis, Indiana; Mountlake Terrace High School in Mount Lake

Terrace, Washington; and Lincoln High School in Stockton, California, as well as Cornerstone Christian College Prep Day and High School have in common?

Cornerstone Christian College Prep Day and High School, as well as the others, are schools with administrative leadership, such as teachers who strongly believe

in Howard Gardner's theory of multiple intelligences as outlined in his book *Frames of Mind* and have convinced their students, many of them minorities and poor, that each of them is brilliant and gifted. The result is that school achievement has skyrocketed beyond any comparable school in their locales. These schools have subscribed to the belief that to view students as multifaceted individuals increases the demand for academic achievement and repudiates any narrow theoretical beliefs concerning intelligence as a property of genetics only, leaving minorities and the poor terminally assigned to sanctioned underachievement.

The purpose of this chapter is to present a critical examination of one particular aspect of Howard Gardner's excellent treatise on multiple intelligence that fails to fully challenge the notion of assigning IQ numerical symbols. This historically has perpetuated an educational caste system that relegates large numbers of minority and poor people to dismal futures because of perceived lack of intellectual ability. A view of intelligence that is not malleable tends to fuel debilitating suspicions of intellectual inferiority, as was expressed by Aronson, Fried and Good, (2001). The focus question is whether Howard Gardner went far enough in his book *Frames of Mind* to eradicate all vestiges of educational disenfranchisement, or did he waffle by agreeing in part that IQ numerical symbols are useful in predicting student success in school?

Frames of Mind by Howard Gardner and the overwhelming attention, as well as success stories, that have been generated by educators who have applied his theory, goes a long way in refuting racist intellectual stereotyping such as was the case in Richard Herrnstein and Charles Murray's *The Bell Curve* (Herman, 1994). The thought that intelligence is a fixed phenomenon determined solely by genetics and not by other factors has been used to perpetuate a racist caste system that, even in the early years of the twenty-first century, continues to strengthen rather than challenge underachievement in minority and poor students.

While many disenfranchised children have benefited from Howard Gardner's theory of multiple intelligences, once the door was open to rethinking the nature of intelligence, he didn't take full advantage of the opportunity to call for the end to all artificial numerical labeling of intelligence, especially in regards to students. It goes without saying that Gardner is a chief proponent of the right of every human being to not be disrespected by being viewed from a single (g) factor of intelligence. For that reason, it was a disappointing that he would take the position that "the importance attached to the number (IQ) is not entirely inappropriate; after all, the score on an intelligence test does predict one's ability to handle school subjects, though it foretells little of success in later life" (Gardner, 1983).

Applying the theory of multiple intelligences has had successes with all children, especially minorities and poor, such as is the case at Key Learning Community in Indianapolis. This demonstrate that the IQ score cannot accurately predict every child's ability to achieve in school. In a climate of multiple intelligences, those students who had traditionally been underserved by traditional views of intelligence achieved and flourished when IQ was viewed as a multidimensional entity.

Teacher expectations are often too strong of a force for students to overcome, especially when those expectations are enforced by narrow, racist views of IQ. Gardner uses *Frames of Mind* to inform and influence those human potential practitioners, such as educators, to view the nature of IQ as multidimensional, which by definition forces teachers to view students as multifaceted human beings.

Teachers who read Gardner's statement acquiescing to the importance of IQ numerical symbols may have existing erroneous belief systems about student intellectual ability bolstered, especially in the case of minority and poor children. This only tends to further sanction and excuse poor academic success. Gardner should have confronted the act of putting faith in arbitrary numbers that negatively stereotype children and assign them to lesser achievement by virtue of lower teacher expectations, as practices that are totally inappropriate and inhumane.

Many educators, psychologists, and counselors strongly agree with Gardner's theory of multiple intelligences; however, he alienated some of his staunchest supporters by refusing to venture far enough to totally dismantle the practice of assigning IQ numerical symbols that are derived from narrowly viewing intelligence as only the properties of linguistics and logic. This can be construed by some as a form of co-signing that will continue to alienate the students from their giftedness, and in turn alienate them from meaningful academic and life success. The threats from these types of stereotypes are too powerful for children or parents to overcome, especially when teachers consider such practices as reliable in, as Gardner says, predicting how well students can handle school subjects (Gardner, 1983).

Intelligence and humans is too complex and multifaceted to have perceived ability reported in terms of a fixed intelligent quotient. Intelligence is by nature innate and only surfaces when appropriate tasks summon its task-specific abilities. An IQ test cannot address all human intelligence; therefore, any attempt to assign a terminal numerical symbol is totally inappropriate and further perpetuates underachievement in minority and poor students.

Howard Gardner's theory of multiple intelligences is a giant step in the right direction in regards to dealing with all children, especially the minorities and the poor from the human dignity perspective that views intelligence not from a fixed phenomenon but one that is varied and expandable. His theory simply helps to bolster the beliefs of many educators who instead need the courage to believe that all children are capable of meaningful achievement, regardless of ethnicity or poverty issues. Gardner believes that every human being has some of those intelligences, whether they are linguistic, spatial, logical-mathematical, musical, interpersonal, intrapersonal, or body kinesthetic. Of course, since the release of *Frames of Minds* Gardner has identified additional intelligences.

Gardner's theory seriously threatens stereotypical racist views that have been used to relegate far too many children to a life of hopelessness and denied them the vision of needed intellectual ability to improve themselves and their lot in life.

Overt racial discrimination for the most part has been eradicated in the United States; however, racist and sexist thinking, as well as attitudes that are bolstered by erroneous knowledge, such as is promulgated in *The Bell Curve* must be challenged and confronted squarely in the face. It appears that Gardner was trying to appease his follow psychologists who are threatened by his theory of multiple intelligences that opposes the traditional view of intelligence that was the result of the work of Charles Spearman and others (Reynolds, Livingston, and Willson, 2006). . The fact remains that IQ numerical symbols lock a sizable number of students out of any meaningful pursuit of true academic success. Gardner's refusal to challenge the use of these numerical intelligence symbols can be construed as a partial cosigning of a system that continues to relegate minority and poor students to perpetual miseducation and underachievement.

A huge injustice is done to minority and poor students by the stereotypical behavior of fixing and labeling IQ, for the process itself is suspect and does more to bring about miseducation than achievement. While Howard Gardner is to be applauded for confronting the theory that there is only one general type of intelligence, it was a disappointment that he didn't go further by calling for the end to all fixing of intelligence through numerical symbols, especially in children.

It is no secret that minorities and poor children have not benefited from standardized testing as much as some races, for the vestiges of slavery that assigned blacks to subhuman intelligence is further kept alive by the practice of assigning intelligence on a fixed basis as opposed to an expansive notion. Racist and inhumane expectations result when teachers take IQ testing that purports to predict a student's success in school and use it to fix expectations as to what levels children are allowed to learn and achieve.

Gardner discussed the fixing of IQ through numerical symbols when he said, "IQ scores do have some relevance for they are used to predict a student's success in school." Many would differ with him in that regard and would argue that when given the opportunity, he should have boldly removed any relevance of intellectual stereotyping which leaves African Americans, Hispanics, Native Americans, and poor children limited to the extent to which they experience the dignity of achieving because an arbitrary score has convinced their teachers that these minority or poor students cannot learn as well as those with the higher IQ numerical symbols.

Traditionalists who continue to adhere to a narrow definition of intelligence, by their own admission report a constant one deviation difference of fifteen points between whites and blacks in regards to IQ.

Since they also purport that numerical intelligence symbols should have a close correspondence with numerical achievement symbols, it is obvious that inequity in perceived intelligence also produces corresponding inequity in achievement, thus perpetuating underachievement because of the underestimating of student intelligence and academic ability as reported by Reynolds et al. (2006).

Gardner's belief that there is some reliability in the use of numerical symbols for IQ does not harmonize with his overall commitment and passion in regards to multiple intelligences. It is unfortunate that he did not fully challenge the continued use of such traditional practices that can never adequately measure innate intelligence, and further exasperate the process by continuing to assign numerical IQ symbols that give too many teachers the authority to teach some students and deny them the authority to teach others, especially those who are starving for academic achievement and success. .

The Law of Aerodynamics says that bumblebees should not be able to fly; however, they have been doing so for eons. Like the bumblebee, Young Men of Color and the rest of humanity, must perceive and embrace their inherent power and inherent resiliency with diverse perceptions that emphasize multiplicity in thought in order to experience new abilities and find new solutions in response to challenges and setbacks in life.

CHAPTER NINE

THE TRANSFORMATIVE POWER OF RESILIENCE ENVIRONMENTS

"Removing Personal Experiences and Preference from Teacher Expectations in the Instruction of Young Men of Color"

I n light of the fact that most view resilience as a dynamic, multidimensional construct that uses mulit-directional interaction between the person and his or her environment, (Luther et al. 2000; Masten, 2001)., Dr. Dowdell-Underwood then offers strategies for developing and implementing verbal, intellectual, social, emotional, physical, and spiritual environments that nurture resilience and empower it, as opposed to ignoring its existence and its ability to cause all people, including Young Men and Young Women of Color to overcome the plethora of formidable challenges that oppose their success in education and in life.

Resilience in the Bumblebee is argued in regards to the person-centric paradigm for finally stopping the endless bleeding of Young Men of Color. Despite its heavy and large body, the bumblebee is able to fly-defying the Law of Aerodynamics. The bumblebee flies because its' Inherent Power and Inherent Resilience, due to intentional adversity that it faces as a way of life, is greater than its challenges, aerodynamics and gravity, included. Cumulative evidence indicates a cultural bias in regards to teacher expectations that negatively impacts the academic achievement of poor and minority students.

An examination of research indicates that poor and minority students experience lower academic achievement in comparison to white middle and upper class students. According to Charles Sykes, schools today tend to look upon disadvantage minority students as though they were on the verge of mental breakdown, to be protected from any undue stress. Ideas such as this, if allowed to proliferate, significantly stall the advancement of minorities (Sykes, 1995).

Neither race nor poverty can be acceptable excuses for underachievement. The urban educational centers in America continue to reflect historical cultural beliefs that traditionally ignored the plight of the poor and made it illegal in many sections of the country for an African American to be taught to read. According to Juan Williams, a nationally respected reporter for the *New York Times*, today's civil rights movement is being played out in the schools of America where poor and minority children cannot expect to achieve a descent education (Williams, 2007).

Bumblebees Can Fly focuses on personal strength and personal resources that every human being, including Young Men of Color possess by virtue of their humanity, despite their formidable challenges of discrimination, marginalization, and disenfranchisement in life.

In Bumblebees Can Fly, Dr. Oscar Dowdell-Underwood challenges Young Men of Color, as well as parents, educators, churches, government, policymakers, community leaders, and nonprofit organizations to expand opportunity for Young Men of Color and other marginalized people by using their Inherent Power and Personal Resiliency to adopt a SYSTEMATIC PROTOCOL by which they can effectively overcome life challenges by recognizing the strength and resilience that is a major component of the Inherent Power that all people, by virtue of their humanity, possess without needing to seek approval of others.

A climate of underachievement in the education of America's poor and minority children is proof of a cultural divide in regards to educational expectations. Historically, this disenfranchisement has existed for several centuries. The poor and minorities have not benefited from educational initiatives, such as No Child Left Behind (NCLB) as much as their white, middle and upper class counterparts. Yet, there are schools in urban centers where cultures of high teacher expectations and high student achievement exist. These educational cultures must be examined to target motivational climates that they have in common that serve to challenge old belief patterns concerning the achievement of poor and minority children (Cotton, 1989).

In light of the fact that most view resilience as a dynamic, multidimensional construct that uses mulit-directional interaction between the person and his or her environment, (Luther et al. 2000; Masten, 2001)., Dr. Dowdell-Underwood then offers strategies for developing and implementing verbal, intellectual, social, emotional, physical, and spiritual environments that nurture resilience and empower it, as opposed to ignoring its existence and its ability to cause all people, including Young Men and Young Women of Color to overcome the plethora of formidable challenges that oppose their success in education and in life.

Most researchers agree that culture manifests itself through climate, and in and of itself can only be qualitatively measured. However, climate which is the surface manifestation of culture can be quantitatively assessed (Cox, Hutchinson, King & McAvoy, 2005). The variable of culture must be examined to ascertain the extent to which academic underachievement is the result of cultural bias and disenfranchisement. Few studies have looked beyond the family and sociological demographics to examine how other variables influence achievement among Black students (Ford, 1993, pp. 47–66).

Until beliefs that lower academic expectations are challenged in regards to how they are expressed in the instructional process, America cannot seriously expect to see meaningful progress across the board in narrowing the achievement gap.

When underlying cultural beliefs, norms, and values regarding educational expectations for poor and minority children through the instructional process are systematically addressed, it would be logical to assume that subsequent achievement will follow. Research consistently reveals that schools that establish high expectations for all students—and provide the support necessary to achieve these expectations—have high rates of academic success (Rutter, Maughan, Mortimore & Outston, 1979). Culture is perpetuated by beliefs and perception, which orders climate and motivation. Behavior such as achievement is the result of the climate which nurtures the invisible variable of culture (Cinq Mars, 2006).

Educational Reform, among other things, must seek to establish motivating climates that challenge erroneous stereotypes and belief paradigms concerning perceived ability of poor and minority students. If culture has the power to manifest climate attitudes and behavior, then the inverse can occur where a change in climate can positively affect a change in culture. Thus, classrooms, schools, and families that have been learning-disenfranchised for a sizable number of poor and minority children can become centers of achievement and empowerment.

Research consistently demonstrates a crucial relationship between culture issues such as teacher expectations and student achievement. Low–achieving students are less-likely to be asked cognitive complex questions that could strengthen their intellectual development. Students have a way of internalizing educational culture through instructional climate; therefore, they will be less motivated to learn and achieve (Team, 2006).

Teachers may have the highest altruistic intentions for their students; however, the fact remains that their belief system is shaped by the culture that was native to them. It is from this culture, not teacher methodology programs, that behavior, including instructional practices will surface. The performance of their teaching duties can never be separated from the culture that has shaped their unconscious belief paradigm concerning the education of poor and minority children. Redemptive environments have the power to monitor the framework in which teacher expectations are expressed in the instructional process. Longitudinal studies support Redemptive environments have the power to change in how teacher expectations are communicated can predict changes in how students achieve, beyond effects accounted for by previous achievement and motivation (Eccles & Jissim, 1992, pp. 947–961).

Objectives

1. Remove the power of teacher expectation from the domain of experience -based practices, placing it under the domain of evidence-based instructional practices. But more importantly, balance the power and influence of teacher expectations by placing as great of emphasis also on student-learner expectations. Teachers have the power to teach, but only learners have the power to decide they will learn.

2. Cause high teacher expectation for student performance and students' personal expectations for achievement to be systematic by placing it under the authority of research-based instructional strategies via the Five Motivational Climates.

3. Equate the Five Motivation Climates (Verbal, Emotional, Social, Intellectual and Physical) with resulting increase in achievement and competency both in the teaching process and the learning process!

4. Identify strategies for forming healthy relationships between students and their potential, teacher leaders-teachers, teacher-students, and school-parent relationships.

5. Foster motivational climates that facilitate sustained instructional excellence in students' belief in their infinite potential to learn and teachers' infinite ability to teach, all in a healthy culture of learning, achievement and competence that is possible by systematically implementation of the Five Environments!

6. Develop an awareness of the five motivational climates that are implemented in the school and classroom educational strategies.

7. Implement an applied research and evaluation schedule to strengthen instruction and measure student achievement.

8. The use of motivational climates strengthens students' learning strategies and capacity and teacher instructional strategies and capacity that help them to systematically express performance expectations in a way that motivates them to improve achievement.

Bumblebees Can Fly:
Inherent Power and Inherent Resiliency

It is important to remove the power of teacher expectation from the domain of experience -based practices, placing it under the domain of evidence-based instructional practices. But more importantly, balance the power and influence of teacher expectations by placing as great of emphasis also on student-learner expectations. Teachers have the power to teach, but only learners have the power to decide they will learn.

CHAPTER TEN

ESTABLISHING RESILIENT VERBAL ENVIRONMENTS

Climate and Instructional Strategies

One must pull from instruction a decision to learn for life and never just for a test; therefore, instruction must be of personal origin and not emanating from another, whether a teacher or parent or others. External instruction is of no value unless it is received and valued internally. Better instructional perceptions will bring about better learning perceptions and result in greater resiliency and use of personal, inherent power to engage systematically in pursuit of desired goals, and greater student achievement and competency.

The Verbal Climate:

Resilience: Personal Power and Personal Strength that resides in the person. Resilience is the ability to bounce back, rebound, and come back from adversity, stronger, healthier, and better than before the opposition or challenge; however, resilience works best when it is the result of a personal policy that is not haphazard or random in response to various adverse events. This climate is concerned with not only how teachers communicate high or low academic expectations to students, but just as important or more-so, how students, themselves empower their own learning through auditory, visual, or kinesthetic communication that respects teachers' power to teach, but refuses to ignore students' sovereign right and ability to choose to learn, despite adversarial conditions. Research points to the following telling facts in regards to teacher expectations in regards to perceived student abilities that are communicated through verbal teacher behavior that alienates underperforming students from the motivation that is needed to bring about significant academic growth and competency

(Montgomery School, 2005; Thompson, R. 2007).

Description of Instructional Expectations that Maximize Student Learning Empowerment and Life Resiliency:

1. One must be very systematic in formulation and embracing a personal policy where one's words toward oneself is empowering and never demeaning. One's identity or potential should be enhanced through adversity, never lost. Resilience in the Bumblebee is argued in regards to the person-centric paradigm for finally stopping the endless of bleeding of Young Men of Color. Despite its heavy and large body, the bumblebee is able to fly-defying the Law of Aerodynamics. The bumblebee flies because its' Inherent Power and Inherent Resilience, due to intentional adversity that it faces as a way of life, is greater than its challenges, aerodynamics and gravity, included.

2. Instead of depending on others, whether teachers, friends, or associates to speak kindly concerning one's ability, it is important that everyone set the tone and example for others' dealings with them by how one deals respectfully and empowering with oneself.

3. Since research says that many teachers tend to call on low-performing students less often to answer questions or make public demonstrations. Students must be resilient verbally, intellectually,

socially, emotionally, and physically by volunteering to answer questions or to ask meaningful questions.

4. Many teachers are prone to criticize low-performing students more than high achievers for incorrect responses. In many cases, underachievers receive less praise than high achievers after successful results or correct responses; empowered students must counter this type of adversity with healthy doses of self-affirmation that liberal in healthy acknowledgement of personal abilities and potential.

5. Many teachers tend to praise low-performing students more frequently than high-performing students for giving marginal and inadequate cognitive responses.

6. Many teachers tend to provide low-achieving students with less-accurate and less detailed feedback than high achieving students. Therefore, students must counter this by only using positive self-talk with themselves. Potential responds to expectations!

7. Many teachers tends to interrupt underperforming students more frequently than high-performing students; however, students must keep possession of their power and right to learn by not being afraid to take the risk to answer questions and to believe in the ability to answer correctly, and seeking clarity if they fail. Empowered students never negatively label their potential, but also their effort and need to learn what was previously unknown.

Instructional Strategies:

- Remove the randomness from the decision as to which students are called upon to answer questions. Suggestion: simply pull students name from the Question Box. Students must protect their right and ability to learn to removing all fear of answering questions and constructively listening and focus during the instructional process.

- Be intentionally as critical of high-performing students' incorrect responses as they are low-performing students' incorrect answers.

- Students' empowerment to learn must be protected by seeing failure through the lens of greater resiliency and clarity by receiving better understanding and awareness.

- Students must never abdicate the right of students to choose to learn and teachers must never abdicate their right to teach.
- Students need to learn to provide liberal amounts of verbal self-encouragement daily, especially prior to learning or the introduction of new and more challenging cognitive curriculum, or prior to exams. The teacher's voice, whether perceived by students or the teachers, themselves, needs to be synonymous with "Student-Learning and Achievement Empowerment, as opposed to equating it with discipline, only. This encourages and strengthens learning in all students, including those who have experienced historical underperformance. Schools that foster high self-esteem and that promote social and scholastic success reduce the likelihood of emotional and behavioral problems (Rutter, 1979).
- Teachers need to structure lesson design and students need to adopt a personal protocol for learning and success for teacher-student questioning, sharing, and actions that encourage the efforts of all students, high achievers and low achievers, alike.
- Structure the learning environment, whether external or internal so that it encourages students to share their personal views in regards to the aspects of the curriculum that is being discussed.

Bumblebees Can Fly: Inherent Power and Inherent Resiliency

Students need to learn to provide liberal amounts of verbal self- encouragement daily, especially prior to learning or the introduction of new and more challenging cognitive curriculum, or prior to exams. The teacher's voice, whether perceived by students or the teachers, themselves, needs to be synonymous with "Student-Learning and Achievement Empowerment, as opposed to equating it with discipline, only.

CHAPTER ELEVEN

ESTABLISHING RESILIENT INTELLECTUAL ENVIRONMENTS

Climate and Instructional Strategies

Climate and Instructional Strategies:

One must pull from instruction a decision to learn for life and never just for a test; therefore, instruction must be of personal origin and not emanating from another, whether a teacher or parent or others. External instruction is of no value unless it is received and valued internally. Better instructional perceptions will bring about better learning perceptions and result in greater resiliency and use of personal, inherent power to engage systematically in pursuit of desired goals, and greater student achievement and competency.

The Intellectual Climate:

This climate is concerned with how high expectations are communicated for self or received and perceived from others through engaging self in cognitive inquiry and tasks; always expecting the best of oneself and others; never putting negative labels on one's identity because of disappointment or failure, but ascribing it to effort and thus a decision to be more resilient in the future.

Research indicates that students who are perceived as high achievers are routinely asked questions of greater cognitive difficulty, whereas low-performing students are asked only minimal questions. This practice furthers the achievement gap because students tend to adopt as their own expectations those that teaches hold of them. Without appropriate beliefs in their own ability to do cognitively challenging tasks, students will not find the desire and confidence needed to make substantial intellectual growth (Accel Team, 2006.; Newman & Wehlage, 1992; Pathways Home, 1995)

Lower-achieving students are more likely to be asked lower-level cognitive questions that require only factual recall, which limits their access to rigorous instruction and denies them the opportunity to engage in challenging academic pursuits. Motivation to learn and consequential academic performance suffers because low achieving students begin to feel less capable than high achieving students who have more opportunities to respond or respond in more cognitively challenging ways. Research indicates that engaging low-achieving students in a challenging, speed-up as opposed to a slowed-down, remedial curriculum produces positive academic and social outcomes (Slavin, 1979). When a poor, inner-city school established a college core curriculum, over 65 percent of its graduates went on to higher education—up from 15 percent before the program began (California Department of Education, 1990).

Description of Instructional Expectations:

1. Students must demand of themselves, and teachers must of themselves unapologetic excellence and maximum achievement and instruction.

2. Students must demand more of themselves than what has been assigned by teachers. This needs to be done routinely and

systematically so that new potential and solutions continue to surface in their education and in life.

3. Students who are perceived as low achieving are often seated further from the teacher than are high achievers. Therefore, regardless of whether elementary, middle, high school, or college, students should seat themselves as close to the teacher as possible. It empowers motivation, perception, and achievement.

4. Teachers tend to wait less time for low achieving students to answer questions. Therefore, students need to protect their personal, inherent power and potential by volunteer

5. Teachers tend to pay less attention to low achieving students in academic situations than to high achievers; therefore, students must take the initiative and responsibility to protect their personal, inherent power and potential by having a laser focus, intentionally, determined to learn whatever is being taught.

Instructional Strategies:

- Although there are ability differences among students, all students should be given the respect of cognitive tasks that cause them to experience intellectual growth.

- Teachers must be held accountable for teaching at maximum levels or excellence in a myriad of ways, whether auditory, visual, or kinesthetic. Teachers must hold all students, and students must hold themselves accountable for demonstrating intellectual growth through completion of all academic tasks and meeting minimum time lines.

- Teachers must give eye contact to all students, and students must be laser focused while engaged in teaching or inquiry activities, being careful to not send messages of intellectual disrespect by looking away or shifting focus.

- Teachers must make sure that there is equitable delivery of the curriculum to all students, regardless of their perceived intellectual ability. Students must protect their personal power to achieve and learn by refusing to assign others, whether teachers or parents their sovereign, inalienable right and power to learn whatever they need or choose to learn.

Like the bumblebee, everyone has something that works against his or her potential; however, also like the bumblebee, all people have deep deposits of inherent power which allows them to do what otherwise would be impossible. Teachers must hold all students, and students must hold themselves accountable for demonstrating intellectual growth through completion of all academic tasks and meeting minimum time lines.

CHAPTER TWELVE

ESTABLISHING RESILIENT SOCIAL ENVIRONMENTS

Climate and Instructional Strategies

The Social Climate:

Resilience: Personal Power and Personal Strength that resides in the person. Resilience is the ability to bounce back, rebound, and come back from adversity, stronger, healthier, and better than before the opposition or challenge; however, resilience works best when it is the result of a personal policy that is not haphazard or random in response to various adverse events. This climate is concerned with how high or low expectations are communicated, whether personal or received from others. It focuses on how abilities are perceived through the degree to which efforts are praised, encouraged and coached to succeed at higher levels of academic achievement and life success. Research reveals that many underperforming students transform into high achievers when a teacher or significant other consistently expect more of them. People tend to be more comfortable around others who match perceived expectations, whether those expectations are high or low. On the other hand, people tend not to be as comfortable around those who don't meet our expectations (Cooper, 2007).

Conveying high expectations to students occur in several ways, one of the most important is through personal relationships in which the teacher and other school staff communicate to students the work students do is important. Encouragement from teachers, such as: "I know that you can do it; I won't give up on you" was an important motivator for decisions students made to try harder and achieve more (Howard, 1990).

Instructional Strategies:

- Students must refuse to accept any labels that marginalize their ability to learn, succeed, and achieve.
- Students must view themselves, and teachers must view every student as valuable and important, and communicate that truth through rigorous, academic expectations coupled with liberal encouragement and support.
- Students must protect their personal, inherent power and potential by expressing themselves with themselves or others through strategies that communicate value to themselves and others, by endeavoring to emphasize personal strengths, interests, and abilities.
- Establish a student-student, teacher-teacher, teacher-student covenant relationships that conveys self-worth through high expectations so that in return empower these beliefs to create a culture of and greater resiliency in achievement and success.
- Students must learn to be at peace with themselves, their failure, and potential.

Bumblebees Can Fly:
Inherent Power and Inherent Resiliency

As He did with the bumblebee, GOD has blessed everyone with inherent power, potential and resiliency. Therefore, students must protect their personal right to learn and achieve by systematically refusing to accept any labels that marginalize their ability to learn, succeed, and achieve.

CHAPTER THIRTEEN

ESTABLISHING RESILIENT EMOTIONAL ENVIRONMENTS

Climate and Instructional Strategies

The Emotional Climate:

Resilience: Personal Power and Personal Strength that reside in the person. Resilience is the ability to bounce back, rebound, and come back from adversity, stronger, healthier, and better than before the opposition or challenge; however, resilience works best when it is the result of a personal policy that is not haphazard or random in response to various adverse events.

This climate is concerned with how students communicate high or low expectations to themselves or how teachers communicate these high expectations to students through support and encouragement given to students, which in turn, aides student achievement and competency. All students who receive routine encouragement in regards to their academic pursuits experience more meaningful achievement. Research says that students who are perceived as high achievers are given more support and encouragement from teachers, through smiles, nods, eye contact, and other means (Cotton, 1989,; Stiff, 2001).

In an experiment conducted by Robert Rosenthal and Lenore Jacobson, 20% of school children from 18 elementary classrooms were randomly grouped and assigned to rooms where teachers were told that they were intellectual bloomers. (Holt, Rinehart and Winston, 1968). Teaches were told that these students could be expected to show remarkable gains during the year. As a result, the children in the experiment averaged IQ gains of two points in verbal ability, seven points in reasoning and four points in overall IQ. In other words, due to teacher expectations, those who perceived to be intellectual bloomers, actually bloomed intellectually.

Instructional Strategies:

- Struggles, failure, and adversity are neutralized by personal awareness of possessing personal assets that can constructively respond to adversity and setbacks.
- Although, smiles, nods of approval and support, eye contact, respect, warmth, and caring are important to instruction, learning, and achievement when students receive them from teachers, it is even more important for students to routinely receive the same from and for themselves.
- Although, the assessment aspect of the learning process is important, the strongest emotions of confidence, pride, happiness and euphoria should be experienced when instruction and processing of knowledge and learning new information is occurring.
- In order to protect personal inherent power and resiliency, students need to protect personal inherent power and resiliency to achieve and succeed by always having a picture of an empowered and capable perception of themselves, their abilities, and their future.
- Students must learn how to give greater importance to the euphoria that is experienced during the learning process as opposed to the momentary affirmations that result when they receive feedback

from how they performed on a test or other short-term method of assessment.

- Research points out that students who receive systematic, routine encouragement in regards to their academic pursuits tend to experience greater achievement and success.

- It is necessary for teachers to believe in all students' ability to learn and achieve, but it is even more important that students believe in their own capacity to learn anything and bounce back from failure and setbacks.

- Cultivate a covenant of learning in the classroom where all students know that their welfare is important to the teacher and other students.

- A routine of encouragement and praise as natural aspects of the routine instructional process for teachers as well as students.

- Give all students, low and high achievers alike, the same opportunity to be engaged in higher-order thinking so that they all can experience the dignity that comes with believing that one is literate and competent.

Bumblebees Can Fly:
Inherent Power and Inherent Resiliency

Students must learn how to give greater importance to the euphoria that is experienced during the learning process as opposed to the momentary affirmations that result when they receive feedback from how they performed on a test or other method of assessment.

CHAPTER FOURTEEN

ESTABLISHING RESILIENT PHYSICAL ENVIRONMENTS

Climate and Instructional Strategies

The Physical Climate:

The physical environment should confirm and strengthen all other environments that are part of the learning and achieving process. The verbal, intellectual, social, and emotional environments all converge in the physical environment. It's the physical environment that has the power to wreck or strengthen the ultimate learning environment.

Research continues to reveal that the physical environment where students experience instruction and learning have a great impact not only on student attendance, persistence, teacher retention, community perceptions, but more importantly, student achievement and success. The greatest achievement has been documented to be influenced by the quality and empowering affirmations of the physical environment.

Resilience: Personal Power and Personal Strength that resides in the person. Resilience is the ability to bounce back, rebound, and come back from adversity, stronger, healthier, and better than before the opposition or challenge; however, resilience works best when it is the result of a personal policy that is not haphazard or random in response to various adverse events. Teachers are more excited about teaching and students are more excited about learning in an affirming, attractive, warm, empowering and secure physical environment.

This climate is concerned with how the physical environment communicates high or low academic expectations to students, staff, parents, and the community through observable and physical actions in the physical environment of the school or classroom. Youth who succeed against the odds speak of being respected and of having their strengths and abilities recognized (Pathways Home, 1995). One of the most powerful ways to do this is to display student work in a way that reveal student intellectual ability. The old adage is that a picture is worth a thousand words. All students, both low and high achievers deserve the respect of having their intellectual abilities reflected in their classroom, school and community (McGrew & Evans, 2004, Accel Team, 2006).

The physical grouping and arrangement of students in a school or classroom also reveal expectations teachers have for them. Heterogeneous, cooperative learning groups provide the positive academic and social outcomes that educational reform advocates (Wheelock, 1992; Johnson & Johnson, 1990; Slavin, 1990).

Bumblebees Can Fly:
Inherent Power and Inherent Resiliency

Research continues to reveal that the physical environment where students experience instruction and learning have a great impact not only on student attendance, persistence, teacher retention, community perceptions, but more importantly, student achievement and success. The greatest achievement has been documented to be influenced by the quality and empowering affirmations of the physical environmen

BIBLIOGRAPHY AND KEY REFERENCES

General Understanding of Redemptive or Motivational Climates:

Brattensani, Karen A. (1984). *Student Perceptions of Differential Teacher Treatment as Moderators of Teacher Expectation Effects*. Retrieved from the world -wide web on April 6, 2007 from http://eric.ed.gov/ERICWeb/ Home.portal?_nfpb=true&_pageLabel=Record Detail&E. .

The author revealed that students acquire information about their abilities by observing the differential treatment accorded high and low achievers. They then revise their own achievement expectations and perform according to the expectations perceived.

Hallinger, Philip. (1989). What Makes a Difference? School Context, Principal Leadership and Student Achievement. Retrieved from the world -wide web on April 6, 2007 from http://eric.ed.gov/ERICWebPortal/ Home.portal?_nfpb=true&_pageLabel=RecordDetails & E . . .

The author addresses the role of the school principal in school improvement through secondary analysis of data collected from 98 elementary schools in Tennessee that participated in the School Improvement Incentives Project between 1983 and 1986. This paper explores an instructional leadership model as operationalized in measures of selected school context variables, principal gender, principal instructional leadership, school level instructional climate, and school level instructional organization.

Tauber, R. (1998). *Good or bad, what teachers expect from students they generally get!* ERIC Digest. Washington, DC: ERIC Clearinghouse on Teacher and Teacher Education, ED426985.

Research suggests that teacher expectations can predict changes in student achievement behavior. This Digest discusses the Pygmalion effect, or the idea that one's expectations about a person can eventually lead that person to behave and achieve in ways that conform to those expectations. The Pygmalion effect identifies climate, feedback, input, and output as the factors teachers use to convey expectations. Climate: the socio-emotional mood or spirit created by the person holding the expectation, often is communicated nonverbally (e. g.,smiling and nodding, eye contact, and leaning closer to the student).

Understanding Verbal Motivational Climates:

The Montgomery School. (2005). *Strategies for Communicating High Expectations to Students. Response Opportunities.* Retrieved on March 27, 2007 from http://www.montgomeryschoolsmd.org1departments/development/diVersity/tip8.pdf

This article discussed the fact that research consistently demonstrates that teachers ask high achieving students more cognitively complex questions than are asked of low achieving students. In fact, lower achievers are more likely to be asked factual recall questions, which negatively affects how these students perceive their cognitive abilities.

Thompson, R. (2007). *Pygmalion Motivation.* Retrieved on April 2, 2007 from http://www.mindtools.com/pages/article/newLDR_88.htm.

This article discusses the Pygmalion Effect in a manner that helps the reader think about and understand how one's expectations of other people can influence or motivate those peoples' performance.

The Pygmalion argument states that by setting and communicating high expectations for performance, one can motivate better performance from people one may lead or manage. Of course, the inverse is true in terms of low performance expectations.

Understanding Intellectual Motivational Climates:

Accel Team. (2006). *How Teacher Communicate Expectation*. Retrieved on April 2, 2007 from http://www.accelteam.com/pygmalion/prophecy 06.html.

Teachers communicate expectation by where students are seated in the classroom, along with what kind of distance the teacher keeps between her or him and students. The article went on to discuss the importance of how much attention the teacher pays to a student in academic

Newman, F. and Wehlage, G. (1992). *Five Standards of Authentic Instruction*. Retrieved on April 2, 2007 from http://69.20.125.200/channel/workshops/socialstudies/pdf/session6/6,AuthenticInstruction.pdf.

Authors discussed what types of instruction engage students in using their minds well. A framework developed at the University of Wisconsin's Center on Organization and Restructuring of Schools may be a valuable tool for teachers in regards to research that attempts to help students answer complex questions.

Pathways Home. (2005). *High Expectations*. Retrieved on April 2, 2007 from http://frontrangeboces.org/resources/High%20Expectations.doc

This article is a summary of the North Central Regional Educational Laboratory's research on the high expectation phenomena in schools in regards to support that is given to students to facilitate achievement. The article noted the influence of support given to successful schools in regards to principal and teacher high expectations, as well as how students can experience resiliency from poor achievement, in particular in the case of at-risk students.

Understanding Social Motivational Climates

Cooper, G. (2007). *Teaching Effectiveness Program.* Retrieved on March 28, 2007 from http://tep.uoregon.edu/resources/librarylinks/articles/highexpect.html.

Discussion of how high expectations are communicated from teachers to students in order to encourage student academic success.

Cooper, G. (2007). *Communicating High Expectations to Students.* Retrieved on March 28, 2007 from http://tep.uoregon.edu/resources/librarylinks/articles/highexpect.html.

Cooperative learning techniques set high expectations for students. The article stresses that this arrangement allows students to work in groups collaboratively, strengthening self -esteem through successful problem solving.

Understanding Emotional Motivational Climates:

Cotton, K. (1989). *Expectation and Student Outcomes.* Retrieved on April 5, 2007 from http://www.nwrel.org/scpd/sirs/4/su7.htm1

The author quotes the following from George Bernard Shaw's Pygmalion, "The difference between a lady and a flower girl is not how she behaves, but how she's treated." The author then presents an exhaustive study in regards to school and teacher expectations and discusses the origin of how various teacher expectations are acquired.

Stiff, L. (2001). *Beliefs and Expectations*. Retrieved from the worldwide web on April 5, 2007 from http://www.nctm.org/about/content. aspx?id.=1032

The author discusses data from a survey of seventh through twelfth graders conducted by the Metropolitan Life Survey of American Teachers 2001.

Key Elements of Quality Schools: The article reveals that of the African American and Hispanic students polled, their perceptions for their futures were twice as high as were their teachers' views. The article stressed that low income and minority students were less likely to report that teachers helped them prepare for their futures.

Understanding Physical Motivational Climates

Accel Team. (2006). How Teachers Communicate Expectation. Retrieved from http://www.accelteam.com/pygmalion/prophecy_06.html.

This article revealed that teachers communicate their expectations for students in a variety of ways including physical arrangement of student seating and physical distance that is kept between the teacher and student.

McGrew, K. and Evans, J. (2004). *Expectations for Students with Cognitive Disabilities: Is the Cup Half Empty or Half Full? Can the Cup Flow Over?* Retrieved on April 5, 2007 from http://education.unm.edu/nceo/onlinePubs/synthesis55.html.

The author notes that several questions must be raised in order to make informal decisions about the best instruction and assessments for students with cognitive disabilities. One question is how students with cognitive disabilities may be expected to achieve the same level of proficiency as other students. Another question that was posed is whether failure to meet proficiency is due to the students' cognitive disability or lack of appropriate instruction. The final question answered is what effects to teacher expectations have on student achievement.

Bibliography

Accel Team. (2006). *How Teacher Communicate Expectation.* Retrieved on April 2, 2007 from http://www.accelteam.com/pygmalion/ prophecy_06html.

Brattensani, K. (1984). *Student Perceptions of Differential Teacher Treatment as Moderators of Teacher Expectation Effects.* Retrieved on April 6, 2007 from http://eric.ed.gov/ERICWeb/Home. portal?_nfpb=true&_pageLabel=Record Detail&E.

Brophy, J. (1983). "Research on the Self-Fulfilling Prophecy and Teacher Expectations." *Journal of Educational Psychology* (75) 5 (October 1983b): 632–661 (ED 221 530).

Cooper, G. (2007). *Teaching Effectiveness Program.* Retrieved on March 28, 2007 from http://tep.uoregon.edu/resources/librarylinks/articles/ higihexpect.html.

Cotton, K. (1989). *Expectation and Student Outcomes.* Retrieved on April 5, 2007 from http://www.nwrel.org/scpd/sirs/4/su7.html.

Edmonds, R, (1979). Effective Schools for the Urban Poor, *Educational Leadership* 37/1 (October 1979a): 15–24.

Hallinger, P. (1989). *What Makes a Difference? School Context, Principal Leadership and Student Achievement.* Retrieved on April 6, 2007 from http://eric.ed.gov/ERICWebPortal/Home. portal?_nfpb=true&_pageLabel= RecordDetails&E . . .

Kirby, S. (2012). Center for American Progress, *The Top 10 Most Startling Facts About People of Color and Criminal Justice in the United States.* Retrieved on March 11, 2014 from http://www.americanprogress. org/issues/race/news/2012/03/13/11351/the-top-10-most-startling- facts-about-people-of-color-and-criminal-justice-in-the-united- states/

A Look at the Racial Disparities Inherent in Our Nation's Criminal-Justice System

(Montgomery School. 2005). *Strategies for Communicating High Expectations to Students, Response Opportunities.* Retrieved on March 27, 2007 from http://www.montgomeryschoolmd.org1department/ diversity/tip8.pdf

McGrew, K. and Evan, J. (2004). *Expectations for Student Cognitive Disabilities: Is the Cup Half Empty or Half Full?* Can the Cup Flow Over? Retrieved on April 5, 2007 from http://education.unm.edu/ nceo/onlinePubs/synthesis55.html.

Newman, F. and Wehlage, G. (1992). *Five Standards of Authentic Instruction.* Retrieved on April 2, 2007 from http://69.20.125.200/ channel/workshops/socialstudies/pdf/session6/6, AuthenticInstruction.pdf.

Pathways Home. (2005). High *Expectations.* Retrieved on April 2, 2007 from http://frontangeboces.org/resources/High%20Expectations. doc

Rosenthal, R., and Jacobson, L. (1996). "Teachers' expectancies; Determinants of pupils' IQ gains." *Psychological Reports (1)* 115–118.

Rosenthal, R., and Jacobson, L. (1968). *Pygamalion in the classroom: Teacher expectation and pupils' intellectual development.* New York: Holt, Rinehart & Winston.

Rutter, M., Maughan, B., Mortimore, P., and Outston, J. *Fifteen Thousand Hours: Secondary Schools and Their Effects on Children.* Cambridge, MA: Harvard University Press, 1979.

Slavin, R. (1979). *Effects of Individual Learning Expectations on Student Achievement* No. 288. Baltimore MD: Center for Social Organization of Schools, John Hopkins University, 1979b (ED 189 118).

Stiff, L. (2001). *Beliefs and Expectations.* Retrieved on April 5, 2007 from http://www.nctm.org/about/content.aspx?id.=1032

Tauber, R. (1998). *Good or bad, what teachers expect from students they generally get!* ERIC Digest. Washington, DC: ERIC Clearinghouse on Teacher and Teacher Education, ED426985.

Thompson, R. (2007). *Pygmalion Motivation.* Retrieved on April 2, 2007 from http://www.mindtools.com/pages/article/newLDR_88.htm

CPSIA information can be obtained
at www.ICGtesting.com
Printed in the USA
BVOW08s1001040418
512448BV00003B/358/P